# The White Mountains
*Names, Places & Legends*

# The
# White Mountains

## *Names, Places & Legends*

*by*

John T. B. Mudge

The Durand Press

© 1992 by John T. B. Mudge
All rights reserved
Published by The Durand Press
374 Dogford Road
Etna NH 03750

Library of Congress cataloging in progress
ISBN 0-9633560-0-3

Printed in the United States of America by BookCrafters
Typesetting and design by LaserLab, Hanover, New Hampshire

Maps by John T. B. Mudge, © 1992 by The Durand Press

Cover Illustration: *Presidential Range from Jefferson Highlands*. Oil painting by Edward Hill. New Hampshire Historical Society Collection.

Frontispiece: *The White Mountains from Randolph Hill*.
From a painting by Homer D. Martin. From the author's collection.

## To My Parents,

who, in 1953, bundled four little children
into the 1950 Dodge and traveled
to New Hampshire for the first of many
vacations in the White Mountains.

God, give me hills to climb
And strength for climbing.
*—Arthur Guiterman, 1871-1943*

# Contents

Acknowledgements .................................................................. ix

Foreword by The Hon. James C. Cleveland ......................... xi

Introduction ........................................................................ xv

Maps of the White Mountains ........................................ xxiii

Selected Dates in White Mountain History ...................... xxix

The White Mountains: Names, Places & Legends ................. 1

Artists and Photographers .................................................. 177

Selected Bibliography ......................................................... 181

About the Author ............................................................... 186

# Acknowledgements

In researching and preparing this book, I was fortunate to have a library of my own to begin with. However, all authors must go to more than one source to complete their research. In particular, I am indebted to the staff of two institutions for their assistance and for allowing me to use their collections.

First, I am grateful to the staff of the Special Collections Department at the Baker Library at Dartmouth College who made numerous trips into the stacks to retrieve materials for me.

Secondly, I am grateful to the staff of the New Hampshire Historical Society for their assistance in obtaining research material and photographs from their archives.

I also wish to acknowledge the cooperation of the Art Institute of Chicago, the Wellesley College Art Museum, and the National Gallery for allowing me to reproduce works of art that are in their collections. I also want to thank Mrs. Nancy Torrey Frueh for the material that she provided me about the path building experiences of her family.

# Foreword

This book is a must read either in whole or in part, by those who, like myself and obviously the author, are truly interested in the White Mountains. The author credits specially his extensive research to the New Hampshire Historical Society and the Baker Library at Dartmouth College. The title of the book *The White Mountains: Names, Places & Legends* pretty well describes the contents.

We are given a fascinating glimpse of how intertwined the history of the White Mountains is with those who visited them in centuries past. In other words, this is not a mere glossary of names and their sources. It is interlaced with the legends and the long history of those who were there before and also the magical charm of the mountains and their allure. The fact is that over the years the White Mountains from earliest times, to quote Jeremy Belknap, have "attracted the attention of all sorts of persons."

Not all of these people were particularly heroic, for example, the worker at Colonel Whipple's farm in Jefferson who stole Nancy's dowry and took off, leaving her to freeze to death when she pursued him into the wilderness of Crawford Notch. And, Darby Field, the first known person to have climbed Mt. Washington, may well have been searching for treasure. The glistening white of its peak and the storied fears of Indians to climb it, may well have lead to rumors of mineral wealth and hidden riches.

For the most part, however, the people who came to these mountains were a rather extraordinary group, a cross-section or microcosm of the diverse names and occupations that reflect the growth of the United States of America yesterday and today; Native Americans and early settlers. Hunters, innkeepers, farmers, foresters, writers, poets, road builders, train builders, scientists, professors, politicians, soldiers, artists, authors, environmentalists (real and fancied) summer residents and on and on, were all here, the known and less well known. They attest in profusion to the special appeal of the White Mountains to successive generations and hopefully many more to come.

A reading of this book makes it quite clear that those who really cherish these mountains should have some special gratitude to bestow on a large group of people and organizations. Many of them are mentioned by the author. Among the most obvious are the Society for the Protection of NH Forests and the Appalachian Mountain Club, and to a lesser degree the Randolph Mountain Club and the New Hampshire Audubon Society.

It is not widely understood but the White Mountain National Forest is administered by the U.S. Department of Agriculture and not, as many think, by the U.S. Department of Interior. This makes a big *difference*.

The Department of Interior holdings are primarily in the West. They are run with an environmental bias, strongly mother-henned by organizations such as the Wilderness Society and the Sierra Club. Our native-grown environmental organizations such as the Appalachian Mountain Club and the Society for the Protection of NH Forests are usually more practical and sensible in a common-sense approach to environmental concerns. The key is to maintain the important principle of multiple use. After all, our forest-based industry depends on the wise harvesting of trees and with it the economic development and numerous jobs in Northern New England. In speaking of multiple use, one must also remember (which the author comments on) that the White Mountain National Forest is within a days drive of one-quarter of the entire population of the U.S.

During my years in Congress I became somewhat of a hero to the Appalachian Mountain Club for getting federal funds to improve and widen Route 16 to boulevard proportions to facilitate access to their cash registers and establishment in Pinkham Notch. The Appalachian Mountain Club also joined the Society in applauding my efforts to add substantial additional holdings to the White Mountain National Forest, particularly in the Sandwich Notch area. (Since then, I have had serious second thoughts about adding to the Forest, however. All it seems to do is to set it up for the over-reaching demands by the Sierra Club and Wilderness Society to lock it up as a wilderness area. This limits its enjoyment to a privileged few environmental elitists and denies access to our already long-suffering forest-based industries.)

The above-mentioned applause rapidly diminished, however, when with my active support, the interstate system was continued through Franconia Notch to improve accessibility to Northern NH. Although we finally worked out an acceptable compromise thanks immeasurably to my Administrative Assistant, Bill Joslin, who was stationed full-time in NH, it wasn't easy. In retrospect the problem was compounded by the Wilderness Society and Sierra Club pushing the Appalachian Mountain Club and Society into somewhat uncharacteristic positions.

There is no question, however, that legitimate and realistic environmental concerns have been absolutely essential to improving and preserving the White Mountains. Legitimate and sensible environmental concerns will continue to be imperative as we go forward into the future.

This book makes the importance of a sensible environmental concern unmistakably clear. It is one of the reasons I enjoyed it and say it's a must read. When one considers the enduring help of the White Mountain National Forest and the contribution to that by the Weeks family of Lancaster, NH, it is reassuring to contemplate the future.

Finally, a word about this book's illustrations. Many of them have not been previously published. One of the base station at the Cog Railroad showing *Old Peppersass* along with a B&M engine is particularly striking. It is one of several pictures taken by Eugene Jones, whose interesting background is detailed by the author in a biographical sketch towards the end of the book. In addition, the colored reproductions are particularly striking.

James C. Cleveland

*New London, NH*
*July 2, 1992*

N.H. State Senate 1952-1962
U.S. Congress 1962-1980

# Introduction

In one of the first publications about the White Mountains, written for the American Philosophical Society in the 18th century, Jeremy Belknap stated:

> The White Mountains in the northern part of New Hampshire have, from the earlieſt ſettlement of the county, attracted the attention of all ſorts of perſons.

This statement is as true today as when it was written. Only our styles of script have changed.

The attraction of the White Mountains of New Hampshire to millions of people has not changed. This "Switzerland of America," these "crystal hills," this vast area of crumpled mountain ranges with ridges and notches, ledges and valleys, and springs and streams, has been a part of American history for longer than any other mountain range.

As these hills have been explored and written about beginning in the 1600's, specific names have been given to them. These are the names of famous and less famous men who preceded us in our visits to these hills. These names and history are the subject of this book.

As today's visitors pass through the mountains, perhaps rapidly on the dry roads of summer or more slowly on the snow covered roads of winter, they are passing in the shadows of Nancy, Carter, and Agiocochook. Watson, Jewell, Edmands, and Osgood are met by the visitor who leaves the asphalt ribbons that surround the mountains and walks into the forests that cover them. Israel, Bumpus, and Hitchcock are waterways that have been named after some of the early visitors to these mountains. But, who are these people and where are these places that will forever belong to them? Here we will find the names of pioneering farmers alongside those of the nation's founding fathers. The names of Native Americans, colonial soldiers, and immigrants who arrived in America after the revolution all live in these hills today. Each name that is found here has a history, a knowledge of which will enhance our collective appreciation of these mountains.

In Ernest Poole's *The Great White Hills of New Hampshire* there is an anecdotal story about two boys growing up on a northern New Hampshire mountain farm. During a very cold winter night their father instructed the boys to go out to the barn and to keep the pigs awake and active. After doing this for a short while, and getting colder with each passing moment, one boy turned to his brother and reportedly said, "God damn the son of a bitch who took these hills from the Indians." In the hardship that they themselves were enduring, these boys did not recognize the achievements of their forebears who had earlier come to these mountains. We will look at the achievements of the men who "took these hills from the Indians."

The poet Ralph Waldo Emerson wrote of these hills and its people, "The God who made New Hampshire taunted the lofty mountains with little men." Emerson was not belittling the pioneers who had come here. He was providing the settlers with the recognition that was due them in tribute to the determination and strength that they exhibited when paired against the hostile and unpredictable environment that they found here. The White Mountains are still hostile and unpredictable. Today, descendants of the early pioneers continue to live here just as descendants of early "summer visitors" continue to return here in the footsteps of their ancestors. The descendants who still live and visit here share a love for these mountains. They share a love for the stories that the forests tell, a love for the anthems that the forests sing, a love for the changing gallery of art that is forever experienced, in good weather and in bad, and a love for the simple fragrance of balsam fir. They share a respect for the power of the mountains. And when they respectfully challenge the summits, they share in a test of their physical powers.

❖ ❖ ❖

Man came to these hills in several stages. The first men here were the Native Americans. In recognition of this the white settlers gave their names to some of the hills and valleys. The next group to come were the hunters and trappers - white colonists. Only after the signing of the 1763 Treaty of Paris, ending the French and Indian war and thereby making it safe for others to settle in northern New England, did pioneers come to farm and make permanent homes in these hills.

With the exception of the fertile river valleys the farming in the White Mountains was not very productive. The pioneer farmers had to clear the land of the virgin forest, and in their first year plant a crop of Indian corn and potatoes between the remaining stumps. Over time, these stumps would be removed, but the quality of the farming was little improved, for the soil was thin, cold, and filled with rocks that had been left indiscriminately by the last glaciers, and which had to be removed in order to make the land even slightly suitable for farming.

In these pioneer farms, beds were made of straw, and the bowls and dishes were more often wooden rather than pewter. Boiled meat, peas or beans, and potatoes comprised the daily meal. An early morning or evening meal consisted of either bean or pea broth, and there were few days when meat was eaten more than once. It was a harsh life that left little room for leisure time. It was a life where the scattered farms were both wholly independent of each other but at the same time, very dependent on each other. These farmers lived in an isolation where they knew that they would have to hunt, fish, and grow everything that they would eat and then would have to build anything else that they needed.

While the end of the French and Indian war made it possible for pioneers to open these woods to farming, the end of another war, the Civil War, resulted in the abandonment of many of these same farms. After that war, many veterans went west to the fertile lands that were opened to them as a reward for their military service. The failure of the veterans to return to their rocky New England hill farms caused the land and buildings to be abandoned and the forest to return to claim them both. In the 19th century some of these farms were purchased by the new and growing group of "summer people" who first visited the hotels and then purchased their own homes. Other farm houses and barns fell down and are today identified only by abandoned cellar holes and stone walls which are stood over by similarly abandoned lilac bushes and apple trees in silent tribute to the labors of the pioneers.

❖ ❖ ❖

The object of this book is the identification of these pioneers: trappers, farmers, guides, scientific researchers, path builders and others. By providing today's White Mountain visitor with some of this information, it is hoped that the visit will be more meaningful and longer remembered.

A few words about the names and places that have been included here are in order. The White Mountains is a vast geographic region. Most of the names that are included are in the area of the "Presidential Range," the most visited area. The importance of the Conway and Franconia areas cannot be overlooked and therefore places and mountains in these areas are described. The wilderness that is found in the Mahoosucs and the Kilkenny necessitates mention of these ranges. Where either historically or geographically important, other places have been identified and described.

Most of the places identified can be easily found on the maps of the area or are referenced in the Appalachian Mountain Club (AMC) guide books. However, the visitor should recognize that the AMC guide book will describe in detail the trails to and from a mountain but not the history of the mountain names. Conversely, this book is not a trail guide and should not be used as one. I have not included here the names of many of the small places, streams and rocks, that do not appear on a map but might appear in the AMC guides. These places would not normally be seen by many visitors and their historical significance is often small. I may have included here names of places that some might consider insignificant, but that was my editorial decision. Where I have found multiple explanations for a name, I have chosen to give all of the stories that I found. I reasoned that in the late 20th century it would be futile to try to discuss with the 19th century explorers and writers as to how they had decided upon a specific name.

There are maps included in this book that are meant to help the reader locate the areas that are being described. For the visitor who is just driving through the White Mountains, you will be able to drive along Route 2 and identify the Ridge of the Castles or Mt.

Starr King. On other roads, you may see Glen Boulder, Nancy's Brook, or in Franconia, the "Old Man of the Mountains." Hopefully, your visit will be more enjoyable if you know the stories about the area that you are passing through. For the visitor who leaves his or her car, you will be able to use this book and its maps, in conjunction with a detailed trail guide, to enhance your enjoyment of the hills by learning more about the path builders who cleared these trails for our collective enjoyment. For the reader who is wondering how tall these mountains are, the text material includes the summit elevations in feet.

❖ ❖ ❖

In doing this research, I met a group of new friends that I will introduce you to in the book. The Reverend Thomas Starr King's epic *The White Hills: Their Legends, Landscape and Poetry*, first published in 1871, brought many people to the White Mountains to see the area about which he had written. These visitors required guide books. A variety of books were published, often in many editions over a period of years, by John Spaulding, Moses F. Sweetser, Henry M. Burt, Edson C. Eastman, and Hugh J. Chisholm. I have quoted from some of these guide books to give today's visitor a feeling for how the mountains were perceived and described by the 19th century visitors. It was then that the mountains were opened up to many visitors, and it was then that the "tourist industry" in the White Mountains reached its historic peak. And lastly, it was during the 19th century that many of the places in the White Mountains were named.

Many White Mountain places were named by the authors of the early guide books. It is ironic that in these writings, the authors were sometimes critical of the names that were here.

For example, Moses Sweetser wrote as follows:

> Men of culture have mourned, for many years, the absurd and meaningless origin and associations of the names of the White Mountains.... The confused jumble of the titles of the main peaks suggests the society of the Federal City and the red-tape and maneuvering of politics and diplomacy, rather than the majesty of the natural altars of New England.... The minor mountains are for the most part named after the farmers who lived near them, or the hunters who frequented their forests. The names in themselves are usually ignoble and it may be questioned whether the avocations of a mountain-farmer or a beaver-trapper are sufficiently noble or so tend to produce high characters as to call for such honors as these.

Before Sweetser, the Rev. Starr King had written of the "wretched jumble" of names found in the White Mountains. The reader will soon find that both Sweetser and King contributed many names to White Mountain places. There are two prominent areas named after King. The reader will have to decide for himself whether Sweetser's efforts at naming these mountains exhibited any greater nobility than the names that he described as ignoble.

❖ ❖ ❖

I have specifically not tried to describe and romanticize the views that are found throughout the White Mountains. This is not a book of "Ohs" and "Ahs" about views. To have tried to write such descriptions would have necessitated the redundant use of adjectives that in the end would not do justice to the view that I would be attempting to describe. Where authored by persons important in the history of the White Mountains, I have quoted descriptions of some views. However, for the most part I prefer to let visitors enjoy the views and take those memories with them. The most sensitive visitors will take many memories, leave only their footprints, and quietly acknowledge the endeavors of others in protecting these forests and mountains.

I have visited and walked through these mountains for the past 40 years. I am not a first generation visitor to these hills. Neither am I a native. And just as you can not turn kittens into muffins, I acknowledge that I never will be a native. However, my affection for these mountains extends beyond specifically enjoying them when I am there. I have acquired a small library of books, prints, and maps, both antique and modern, about the White Mountains, that allows me to return there quickly by looking at the walls of my living room or by pulling a book from the shelf for an evening. This personal collection formed much of the foundation for my research—a project that I never envisioned when I began this collection over twenty years ago.

Today man is the trustee for this natural setting known as the White Mountains of New Hampshire. Our predecessors, who left their names in these mountains, were the trustees of this environment during their lives. Undoubtedly, they made both good and bad decisions in their exploration and development. Of most importance today, we are able to enjoy their decisions and their efforts in the mountains that they have bequeathed to us in trust. As we recognize our indebtedness to these efforts, we must be resolved that our decisions and actions in this environment will be recognized and rewarded by succeeding generations.

I hope that your visit is enjoyable and memorable and that this book contributes to that enjoyment. Lastly, readers are invited to send their comments and suggestions to the author, c/o The Durand Press, 374 Dogford Road, Etna, New Hampshire 03750.

# Maps of
# The White Mountains

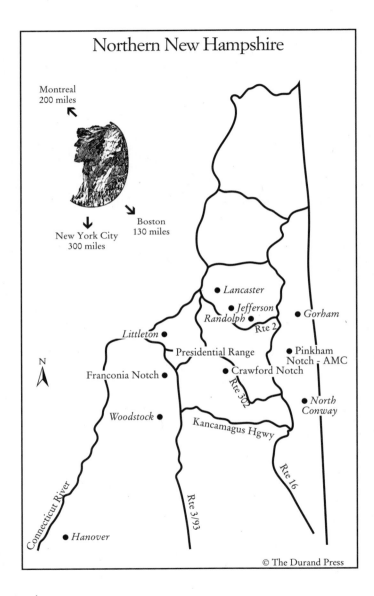

# Northern New Hampshire

Montreal
200 miles

New York City
300 miles

Boston
130 miles

Lancaster

Jefferson

Randolph

Rte 2

Gorham

Littleton

Presidential Range

Pinkham
Notch - AMC

N

Franconia Notch

Crawford Notch

Rte 302

North
Conway

Woodstock

Kancamagus Hgwy

Connecticut River

Rte 16

Rte 3/93

Hanover

© The Durand Press

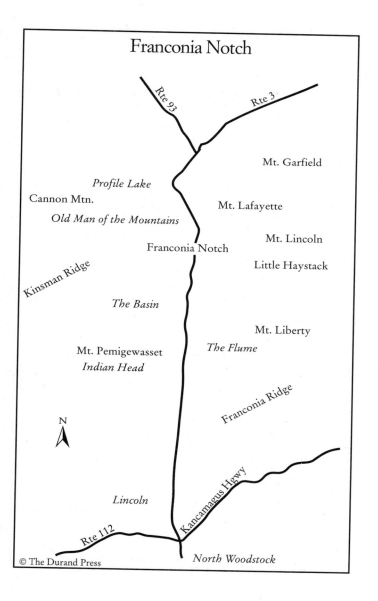

# Franconia Notch

Rte 93

Rte 3

Mt. Garfield

Profile Lake

Cannon Mtn.

Old Man of the Mountains

Mt. Lafayette

Mt. Lincoln

Franconia Notch

Little Haystack

Kinsman Ridge

The Basin

Mt. Liberty

The Flume

Mt. Pemigewasset

Indian Head

Franconia Ridge

N

Kancamagus Hgwy

Lincoln

Rte 112

© The Durand Press

North Woodstock

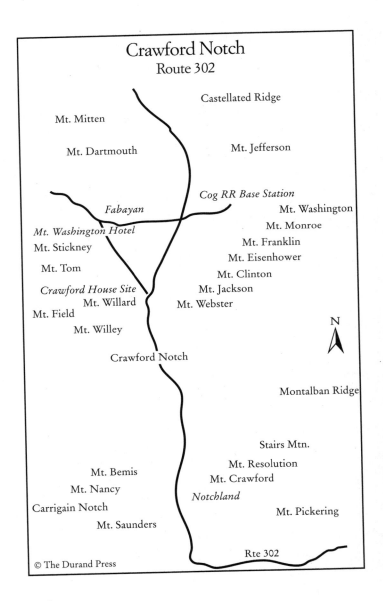

# Crawford Notch
## Route 302

Castellated Ridge

Mt. Mitten

Mt. Dartmouth

Mt. Jefferson

*Cog RR Base Station*

*Fabayan*

Mt. Washington

Mt. Monroe

*Mt. Washington Hotel*

Mt. Stickney

Mt. Franklin

Mt. Eisenhower

Mt. Tom

Mt. Clinton

*Crawford House Site*

Mt. Jackson

Mt. Willard

Mt. Webster

Mt. Field

Mt. Willey

N

Crawford Notch

Montalban Ridge

Stairs Mtn.

Mt. Bemis

Mt. Resolution

Mt. Nancy

Mt. Crawford

Carrigain Notch

*Notchland*

Mt. Saunders

Mt. Pickering

Rte 302

© The Durand Press

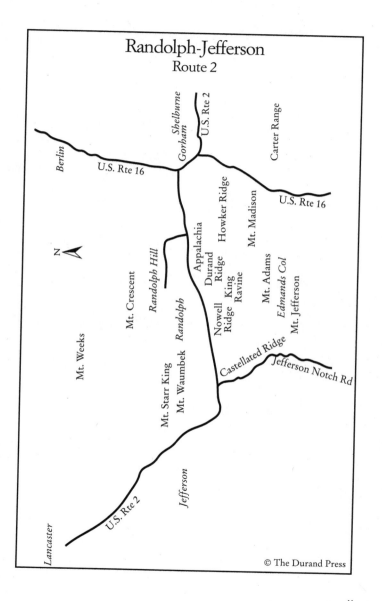

# Randolph-Jefferson
## Route 2

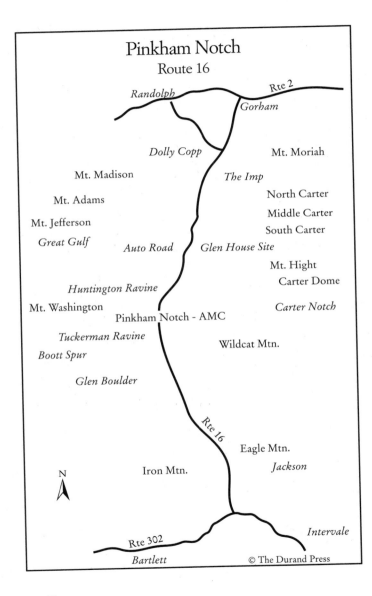

# Pinkham Notch
## Route 16

Randolph

Rte 2

Gorham

Dolly Copp

Mt. Moriah

Mt. Madison

The Imp

Mt. Adams

North Carter

Mt. Jefferson

Middle Carter

South Carter

Great Gulf

Auto Road

Glen House Site

Mt. Hight

Carter Dome

Huntington Ravine

Mt. Washington

Carter Notch

Pinkham Notch - AMC

Tuckerman Ravine

Wildcat Mtn.

Boott Spur

Glen Boulder

Rte 16

Eagle Mtn.

Jackson

N

Iron Mtn.

Intervale

Rte 302

Bartlett

© The Durand Press

# Selected Dates in
# White Mountain History

1524    The White Mountains are first seen from off of the New Hampshire seacoast by Giovanni da Verrazano.

1629    Chief Passaconaway sells part of coastal New Hampshire to colonists.

1634    First ship masts exported to England from New Hampshire.

1642    Darby Field becomes the first person to climb Mt. Washington.

1679    New Hampshire chartered as a Royal Province.

1712    Baker River massacre.

1763    Treaty of Paris signed ending the French and Indian War, making it possible for settlers to move safely to northern New Hampshire.

1771    Crawford Notch discovered by Timothy Nash.

1776-81    American Revolution.

1784    Jeremy Belknap's scientific expedition to the White Mountains. Belknap names Mt. Washington after General Washington.

1791    Abel Crawford moves to the White Mountains and builds a log cabin near what is today known as Fabyan.

1805    First reported sighting of the "Old Man of the Mountains" in Franconia Notch.

1819    Abel Crawford and Ethan Allen Crawford build the first path up Mt. Washington.

| | |
|---|---|
| 1820 | Group of Lancastrians, guided by Ethan Allen Crawford, ascend Mt. Washington and give names to the surrounding summits. |
| 1821 | Ethan Allen Crawford builds the first shelter at the summit of Mt. Washington. |
| 1826 | The Willey family is killed in the Willey House Slide. |
| 1828 | Abel Crawford and Ethan Allen Crawford build the "Notch House" in Crawford Notch. |
| 1831 | Hayes and Dolly Copp marry and move to the family farm in what is now the Dolly Copp Campground. |
| 1832 | The residents of Pittsburg, New Hampshire form an independent republic, the United Inhabitants of Indian Stream Republic, with its own currency and militia. |
| 1835 | New Hampshire militia is sent "abroad," to Pittsburg, to restore order. |
| 1840 | Tom Crawford completes the Bridle Path to the summit of Mt. Washington. Abel Crawford becomes the first person to ride a horse up Mt. Washington. |
| | Pittsburg, the Indian Stream Republic, incorporated into New Hampshire. |
| 1842 | Webster-Ashburton Treaty signed with Great Britain establishing the location of New Hampshire's section of the border between the United States and Canada. |
| 1846 | Ethan Allen Crawford dies. |
| | Publication of Lucy Crawford's *History of the White Mountains*. |
| 1850 | First artist colony in North Conway established by Benjamin Champney and John F. Kensett. |
| 1851 | Atlantic and St. Lawrence Railroad completed to |

Gorham. The era of passenger trains in the White Mountains begins.

Abel Crawford dies.

1853    Charter granted for the Mt. Washington Carriage (Auto) Road.

1855    Publication of the first White Mountain Guide book, *Historical Relics of the White Mountains* by John Spaulding.

Death of Lizzie Bourne near the summit of Mt. Washington.

1861    Mt. Washington Carriage (Auto) Road completed.

1861-65 United States Civil War.

1866    Construction of Cog Railway begins.

1869    Cog Railway completed.

1869-70 J. H. Huntington spends this winter on the summit of Mt. Moosilauke after failing to get permission to do his research on Mt. Washington.

1870-71 J. H. Huntington spends this winter on the summit of Mt. Washington after receiving the cooperation of the Cog Railway.

1871    Publication of *The White Hills: Their Legends, Landscape and Poetry* by the Rev. Thomas Starr King.

1875    First railroad passes through Crawford Notch.

1876    Appalachian Mountain Club formed.

1877    Publication starts of "Among The Clouds" on the summit of Mt. Washington.

1881    Hayes and Dolly Copp leave their farm.

1886    AMC publishes Louis F. Cutter's map of the White Mountain Range.

| 1888 | Construction of the Madison Spring Hut on Mt. Madison completed by the AMC. |
|---|---|
| 1899 | An automobile ascends the summit of Mt. Washington for the first time. |
| 1901 | Society for the Protection of New Hampshire Forests formed. |
| 1903 | Forest fires destroy 84,255 acres in northern New Hampshire. |
| 1907 | AMC publishes the first AMC White Mountain Guide. |
| 1908 | Summit House fire on the top of Mt. Washington. |
| 1911 | Passage of the Weeks Act, establishing the creation of the White Mountain National Forest. |
| 1914 | Construction of the AMC hut in Carter Notch. |
| 1915 | The first shelter is built at the Lakes of the Clouds. |
| 1917 | "Among the Clouds" ceases publication. |
| 1928 | Joe Dodge appointed Manager of the AMC Hut System. Dodge retired from this position in 1959. |
| | Society for the Protection of New Hampshire Forests completes public fund raising project to purchase Franconia Notch. |
| 1932 | Construction of the Mount Washington Observatory. |
| 1944 | Monetary Conference held at the Mount Washington Hotel at Bretton Woods. |
| 1967 | Accident on the Cog Railway kills eight people. |
| 1968 | National Trail System Act passed by Congress and the Appalachian Trail becomes the Appalachian National Scenic Trail. |
| 1977 | Last Crawford House hotel in Crawford Notch burns. |

1980    Dedication of the Sherman Adams Building on the summit of Mt. Washington.

1988    The Society for the Protection of New Hampshire Forests and the Nature Conservancy join with the state and federal government to acquire the 39,500 acre Nash Stream watershed north of the White Mountains.

Today    The federal and state governments, local communities and conservation groups join in discussions and projects to preserve and protect the Northern Forest for future generations.

# The
# White Mountains

*Names, Places & Legends*

# ABENAKI RAVINE

The Abenaki Ravine, on the northwest side of Mt. Eisenhower, was named to honor the Native Americans who first inhabited the White Mountains of New Hampshire. All of the Native American names found today in the White Mountains were given to these places by the white man. The Abenaki, the largest group of Native Americans in this area, did not use these names.

The Abenaki people were sometimes called "Nipmucks" or "Fresh Water People." The word Abenaki has also been translated as "Living at the Sunrise," a reference to the fact that these were Indians who lived in the "east." North of the White Mountains lived the "Sokokis," a sub-group of the Abenakis. Another group in the Coos County area was the "Coosucks" derived from "Coos" for pines and "Auke" for place. This group lived in the Connecticut River Valley. The total Native American population of northern New Hampshire was not very large, perhaps 5,000, at the time of the arrival of the Europeans.

The Native American name for Mt. Washington was Agiocochook, translated differently as "Place of the Storm Spirit," "Home of the Great Spirit" and " the Place of the Spirit of the Forest." The entire Presidential Range was known as "Waumbek—Methna" or "Mountains with White Foreheads."

# ABENAKI

The Native Americans never went up into the mountains, and there has been debate as to whether or not the two that accompanied Darby Field on his trip in 1642 went to the summit of the sacred mountain. To appease their Gods that lived on the summits, the Native Americans held fire dances and sacrificed wild game to the fires.

Perhaps the greatest fire atop the summit of Mt. Washington was at the death of the Indian Chief Passaconaway, "The Fearless One." It was Chief Passaconaway who sold parts of coastal New Hampshire to John Wheelwright in 1629. Passaconaway united 17 tribes in central New England into the Penacook conference. Legend has it that at his death at the age of 120 years, a huge sled, loaded with many furs, arrived at his wigwam. The sled, pulled by twenty-four wolves, dashed off to the summit of Agiocochook (now Mt. Washington). At the summit the sled and the wolves went howling off into the wilderness. Chief Passaconaway burst into flames and was carried into the heavens. Today, Mt. Passaconaway in the Sandwich Range remembers this Indian Chief.

South of Agiocochook (Washington) lived the Pequawkets in the Saco River valley from Bartlett to Conway and Ossipee Lake. The Ossipee, "Dwellers on the Pine Tree Lake," were a tribe that lived near Moultonborough. Legend says that the history of this tribe was carved into a tree in hieroglyphics, but that has never been verified.

In western New Hampshire, overlooking the Connecticut River and the green hills of Vermont, is Mt. Moosilauke, "Bald Place." This mountain is now largely owned by Dartmouth College and is used extensively by the Dartmouth Outing Club.

The Abenaki language was a strictly spoken and phonetic

language. Over time and between different groups of these Indians there were different meanings, sometimes great and sometimes subtle, to the words in the language.

Some of the words in the Abenaki language are:

| | |
|---|---|
| Aukee | – high place, mountain, hill |
| Asquam | – broad sheet of water, large lake |
| Cook | – quiet stretch of water |
| Coos | – pines |
| Keag | – fishing place |
| Mag or Mass | – large, big, high |
| Nipi | – lake or pond |
| Saco | – flowing out, outlet |
| Tegu | – river |

From these words are derived many of the Native American place names of northern New Hampshire.

The European settlers learned much from the Native Americans. They learned about the growing of corn, which was not a European vegetable. They learned about pumpkins and squash. They learned about maple sugar products, and they learned how to build birch bark canoes and snowshoes.

## ADAMS, MT.                                     Elevation 5,798

Mt. Adams, a part of the Presidential Range in the White Mountains, has three peaks that are most clearly seen from Randolph. As seen from there, Mt. Adams, named after John Adams the second President of the United States, is the highest peak. To the east of Mt. Adams is Mt. John Quincy Adams, named after the fourth President and the son of John Adams. To the west of Mt. Adams is a lesser peak known as Mt. Sam Adams, named after Samuel Adams of Massachusetts. Sam Adams was a cousin of John Adams and an early leader in the American Revolution.

Among all of the White Mountains, Mt. Adams has achieved a certain distinction by having been identified as one of ten holy mountains of the world by a group that calls themselves the "Atherians." They believe that this mountain is "charged with an alien force." Summer pilgrimages and ceremonies have been held here to charge energy from the mountain out into the world to create peace.

**AGASSIZ, MT. and Agassiz Basin**          Elevation 2,379

Formerly known as Peaked or Picket Hill, Mt. Agassiz is located above and south of the town of Bethlehem. The name honors the Swiss scientist Jean Louis Rudolph Agassiz who was the first person to recognize that New England and the White Mountains had at one time in their geologic history been covered by a continental glacier. Those glaciers contributed greatly to the molding and rounding of the mountains that exist today. Agassiz Basin near Mt. Moosilauke and a second Mt. Agassiz in Switzerland honor the same scientist.

**AGIOCOCHOOK** (See Mt. Washington)

Agiocochook is the Native American name for what is today Mt. Washington, the highest peak in New Hampshire's White Mountains—the "ridge-pole" of New England.

According to legend, the Native Americans did not climb Agiocochook for they believed that its summit was the home of the Great Spirit. Thus, Agiocochook has been variously trans-

*Mt. Washington from Mt. Agassiz.* Photo by Eugene S. Jones. New Hampshire Historical Society Collection.

5

lated as: "Home of the Great Spirit," "The Place of the Spirit of the Forest," and "The Place of the Storm Spirit."

Agiocochook and the other peaks of the White Mountains were first seen in 1524 from off the New Hampshire coast by Giovanni da Verrazano. In 1642, Darby Field from Exeter, New Hampshire, became the first known person to climb the mountain. Field was accompanied by two Native Americans, but the records are uncertain as to whether they climbed all of the way to the summit or whether they stopped and allowed Field to do that by himself. In 1784, after the American Revolution, but before General George Washington became the nation's first President, the mountain was named in his honor by Jeremy Belknap, the leader of the 1784 scientific expedition to the White Mountains.

The early White Mountain Guide books contain many descriptions of the views of and from Agiocochook—Mt. Washington. Perhaps the best description of the view from the summit of this mountain was written by William Oakes in his *White Mountain Scenery* published in 1848:

> In the west, through the blue haze, are seen in the distance the ranges of the Green Mountains; the remarkable out-lines of the summits of Camel's Hump and Mansfield Mountain being easily distinguished when the atmosphere is clear. To the north-west, under your feet, are the clearings and settlements of Jefferson, the waters of Cherry Pond, and farther distant, the village of Lancaster, with the waters of Israel's River. The Connecticut is not visible, but often, at morning and evening, its appearance is counterfeited by the fog rising from its surface. To the north and north-east, only a few miles distant, rise up boldly the great northeastern peaks of the White Mountain range—

Jefferson, Adams and Madison—with their ragged tops of loose, dark rocks. A little farther to the east are seen the numerous and distant summits of Maine.

On the south-east, close at hand, are the dark and crowded ridges of the mountains in Jackson; and beyond, the conical summit of Kearsarge, standing by itself on the outskirts of the mountains; and farther, over the low country of Maine, Sebago Pond, near Portland. Still farther, it is said, the ocean itself has sometimes been distinctly visible. The White Mountains are often seen from the sea, even at thirty miles distance from the shore, and nothing can prevent the sea from being seen from the mountains but the difficulty of distinguishing its appearance from that of the sky near the horizon. Farther to the south are the intervals of the Saco, and the settlements of Bartlett and Conway, the sister ponds of Lovewell, in Fryeburg and still farther, the remarkable four-toothed summit of Chocorua, the peak to the right much the largest and sharply pyramidal. Almost exactly south are the shining waters of the beautiful Winnipesaukee, seen with the greatest distinctness in a favorable day. To the south-west, near at hand, are the peaks of the south-western range of the White Mountains; Monroe, with its two little Alpine ponds sleeping under its rocky and pointed summit; the flat surface of Franklin, and the rounded tops of Mt. Pleasant, with their ridges and spurs. Beyond these, the Willey Mountain, with its high ridged summit; and beyond that several parallel ranges of highwooded mountains. Farther west, and over all is seen the high, bare summit of Mt. Lafayette, in Franconia. At your feet is the broad valley surrounded by mountains, through which wind deviously the sources of the Ammonoosuc, with its clearing at its farther extremity, and the Mt. Washington House; and beyond this, at twenty miles distance, the little village of Bethlehem is dimly visible.

## AIRLINE TRAIL

The Airline Trail ascends Mt. Adams from the Appalachia parking area on Route 2 in Randolph. This was the first trail that followed a ridge-line and not the bottom of the valley. This trail is above treeline for a long period before it reaches the Madison Spring Hut between Mt. Madison and Mt. Adams. For this reason, its builders, Laban Watson and Eugene Beauharnais Cook, gave it this name.

## ALPINE GARDENS

The area above Huntington Ravine, on the eastern side of the summit of Mt. Washington, is known as the Alpine Garden and is accessible by hiking trail or from parking spaces along the Auto Road.

This area is above treeline, and the vegetation is very fragile. For that reason visitors to this area should be very careful with the plant life that grows here and in all other areas above treeline. Hikers should take care to stay on the rocks and not to trample on the fragile soil which can be easily damaged by modern waffle- soled hiking boots. Since this is a National Forest, plant specimens should not be collected without the permission of the U. S. Forest Service.

The Alpine zone, or above treeline area, can best be described as that region where shrubs come to an end. In the Presidential Range this varies from between 4,800 and 5,200 feet above sea level and extends for the 8½ miles from Mt. Madison to Mt. Eisenhower covering an area of 7½ square miles. The less protected areas, often on the northwest facing slopes, have the lower treeline. A combination of exposure, snow depth, and fog frequency determine the treeline. The same vegetation is found here as is found much farther north in Labrador.

These tiny plants were brought here during the last glacial period. After the ice retreated, they found the climate and the soil conditions to be quite hospitable for their very simple needs. One plant, the Dwarf Cinquefoil, is found here and nowhere else in the world.

Black Spruce and Balsam Fir, both large trees when found at lower, sub-alpine elevations, are much dwarfed near treeline. Here, they are found and known as "Krummholz," German for "crooked wood." These Lilliputian trees vary in height from between one and four feet depending upon elevation, are sometimes over 150 years old, and are very difficult to walk through. Hikers should use trails that pass around them.

Jeremy Belknap's early description of the above treeline area reads as follows: "This plain is compofed of rocks, covered with winter grafs and mofs, and looks like the surface of a dry pafture or a common." Dr. Edward Tuckerman, an early visitor and student of this area described the "wide wilderness" that he found here. Other botanists who have come here to study this tiny fragile plant-life are Francis Boott, William Oakes, Jacob Bigelow, and Manasseh Cutler. (See below.)

## AMMONOOSUC RIVER

There are three Ammonoosuc Rivers in the White Mountains. The Upper Ammonoosuc River flows out of the Kilkenny region north of Randolph and Jefferson and joins the Connecticut River in Groveton.

A second and better known stream, The Ammonoosuc River, flows off of Mt. Washington through the Ammonoosuc Ravine and merges with the Connecticut River in Woodsville,

New Hampshire. The headwaters of this river are the Lakes of the Clouds just below the summit of Mt. Washington. This river falls nearly 6,000 feet from its origin before it reaches the Connecticut River. From the base station of the Cog Railway, the Ammonoosuc Ravine Trail closely follows this stream up Mt. Washington to the Lakes of the Clouds. The third Ammonoosuc River is the Wild Ammonoosuc which originates on Mt. Moosilauke and merges with the Ammonoosuc before flowing into the Connecticut River.

Ammonoosuc is an Abenaki word meaning, "Fish Place," "namos" for "fish" and "aukee" meaning "place."

## ANDERSON, MT.                                    Elevation 3,722

John F. Anderson was the Chief Engineer of the Portland and Ogdensburg Railroad which in 1875 completed the railway through Crawford Notch. Mt. Anderson is located between Mt. Nancy and Mt. Carrigain, above and to the west of Crawford Notch. It took more than a year to complete construction of the 18½ miles of railroad through Crawford Notch. The work was completed using hand tools, black powder and horse drawn carts. The near vertical cliff of Mt. Willard required that the engineers construct a shelf of granite blocks to lay the railbed on. Today, more than a century later, the imagination of the Chief Engineer and labors of the workers still survive.

## APPALACHIA

This name has commonly been given to the trailheads in Randolph. The trails on the northern side of the Presidential Range had a common beginning at the Ravine House before it was torn down in 1962. When Route 2 was relocated a parking area, now known as Appalachia, was constructed at the base of the trails. Legend has it that the name is derived from a story about Laban Watson and William Peek watching several boys eating green apples from a tree near the Ravine House. After eating a large number of these apples, the boys appeared to be feeling their effects and Peek amusingly asked: "What's the matter, has the Apple-ache-i-a?"

## APPALACHIAN MOUNTAIN CLUB (AMC)

Organized in 1876 and now headquartered in Boston, the AMC is a non-profit organization concerned with conserving and promoting the diverse outdoor recreational activities that are available in the northeastern United States. The AMC is the oldest organization of its kind in this country. The AMC maintains eight alpine huts for overnight use in the White Mountains in addition to its hostel and information center in Crawford Notch and the north country headquarters in Pinkham Notch, with its bookstore, information center, and overnight accommodations. In addition, the AMC maintains trails, publishes books and magazines about its activities, conducts workshops, youth programs, outdoor research and, when necessary, assists in search and rescue operations for lost or injured hikers.

The AMC huts stretch over a fifty mile distance from Lonesome Lake in the Franconias to the Carter Notch Hut. In 1888, twelve years after the club was founded, construction began on the first hut at the Madison Spring. The Carter Notch hut was built in 1914 and the Lakes of The Clouds was built in 1915. These three huts then formed a "triangle" for hikers to travel between. It was under the management of Joe Dodge that the hut system was expanded to its current size. A 1961 article in the *National Geographic Magazine* by the late Associate Supreme Court Justice William O. Douglas brought word about "The Friendly Huts of the White Mountains" to many more people and resulted in increasing numbers of visitors coming to New Hampshire and using the AMC hut system.

## APPALACHIAN TRAIL

The Appalachian Trail is a 2,135 mile network of interconnecting foot trails from Maine to Georgia. (In local areas the trail often bears a local name and not the national name.) With the enactment of the "National Trail System Act" in 1968, this trail became the first federally protected footpath in the country and was officially designated as the "Appalachian National Scenic Trail." In the White Mountains this trail passes over the Mahoosuc and Carter Ranges, crosses Route 16 in Pinkham Notch, ascends Mt. Madison via the Madison Gulf and Osgood Trails, passes over to Mt. Washington via the Gulfside Trail, and then continues down to Crawford Notch via the Crawford Path. In Crawford Notch the Appalachian Trail crosses Route 302 and then continues over to Franconia Notch, Kinsman Notch, Mt. Moosilauke, and finally to Hanover, New Hampshire, where the trail crosses the Connecticut River to Vermont.

## ARETHUSA FALLS

Located on the Bemis Brook in Crawford Notch are the 176 foot high Arethusa Falls. These waterfalls were reportedly first discovered by Professor Edward Tuckerman. It was later that they were named by Sweetser and Huntington when they visited them in 1875. The name is an allusion to the poem

"Arethusa," by Percy Bysshe Shelley which tells the story of a Greek myth about a beautiful nymph, Arethusa, who is transformed into a fountain. In part, the poem reads as follows:

> Arethusa arose
> From her couch of snows
> In the Acroceraunian Mountains
> From cloud and crag
> With many a jag
> With her rainbow locks
> Streaming among the streams.

The rocks here are very steep and slippery and should not be climbed.

## ARTIST BROOK

This brook is east of the town of North Conway on Mt. Cranmore. The name honors the many artists who came to North Conway in the 19th century and made it a center for their work.

## ATTITASH, MT.                                   Elevation 2,936

Mt. Attitash and the present Attitash Ski area are located in the town of Bartlett. In the last century a group of hikers found a great number of blueberry bushes growing on this mountain. For this reason Sweetser gave it the name Attitash, the Abenaki word for "Blueberry."

## AUTO ROAD, MT. WASHINGTON

The Mt. Washington Auto Road originates at the Glen House Site on Route 16, north of Pinkham Notch and Wildcat Mountain. Today, visitors may either drive their own cars or

take a "stage" (chauffeured van) to the summit of the mountain.

A charter for the road was granted by the New Hampshire legislature in 1853 and survey work was completed the following year. When the contract was awarded it was estimated that the road would cost $8,000 per mile. Construction began in the summer of 1855, and after one year two miles of the road had been completed. In 1857 the financiers building the road ran out of money and construction was stopped. In 1860, when construction was started again, one-half of the road was opened. The road to the summit was officially opened one year later in August 1861.

When the road was first opened users were charged by the mile. If a person was on foot, he was charged 2¢ per mile. A horse and rider was charged 3¢ per mile while a horse and carriage were charged 5¢ per mile. Over the years the road has been widened and improved in order to accommodate the changes from horses and stages to modern cars. In 1899 a Stanley Steamer, manufactured by the "Locomobile Company of America," and driven by Mr. and Mrs. F. O. Stanley, became the first automobile to ascend Mt. Washington. In subsequent years, there have been road races up the Auto Road, and in 1947 there was a gathering of antique cars on the summit of the mountain.

During the history of the auto road, there have been two fatalities. In July 1880, a drunken driver's carriage accidentally overturned and one woman was killed. A second fatality oc-

*View From the Mt. Washington Carriage Road.*
1875 Bierstadt stereoscopic view. From the author's collection.

curred in 1984 when the brakes of a car became over-heated and wore out by the time the car reached the base of the mountain.

Any person using the Auto Road should use caution and follow all of the instructions of the Auto Road personnel.

## AVALANCHE BROOK

Avalanche Brook merges with the Saco River at the Willey House Site in Crawford Notch. The Rev. Starr King renamed this brook, behind the Willey family farmstead, to commemorate the site of the avalanche that destroyed the Willey family in 1826. This brook had formerly been known as Cow Brook.

## AVALON, MT.                                    Elevation 3,430

West of Route 302 in Crawford Notch is Mt. Avalon, named by Moses Sweetser after the hills of Avalon in Newfoundland, Canada. Sweetser wrote that this New Hampshire hill resembled one in Newfoundland. The Avalon Trail ascends this mountain.

## BAKER RIVER

The Baker River flows in a south-easterly direction from the towns of Wentworth and Rumney to the north of Plymouth where it merges with the Pemigewasset River. For the Native Americans, this river was known as "Asquamchamuake," translated differently as the "Salmon Spawning Place" and "Water of the Mountain Place."

---

*The Climb to the Clouds on the Mount Washington Wagon Road.*
A race on the Auto Road. Photographer unknown.
New Hampshire Historical Society Collection.

## BAKER RIVER

This river is named after a Captain Thomas Baker who in 1712 came north from Massachusetts to engage the Indians camped near the Pemigewasset. At this time, before the French and Indian War, the Province of Massachusetts was still claiming the province of New Hampshire. When he came north Baker obtained the assistance of two friendly Indians to lead him to the area near Plymouth. Upon reaching the point where the Pemigewasset and Baker rivers merge, Captain Baker discovered the Indians on the north bank of the stream. As the men were hunting and away, only the squaws, who were planting corn, and the older men were at the camp. Baker and his men surprised the Indians with the attack and many were killed in the massacre. A few surviving Indians fled to seek assistance. After seizing the Indians' abandoned furs and destroying their camp, Baker retreated to the south. Then, in the process of retreating, Baker engaged in a feat of military deception. When stopping for dinner Baker's men built many fires to suggest that they were a large group of soldiers. Later, when the Indians arrived they counted the many fires, and fearing that it was a very large group of soldiers that they were following, the Indians abandoned their attack. For his successful deception of the Indians, the Baker River was named for this pre-revolutionary Massachusetts soldier.

An explanation for Baker's savage attack lies in his personal experiences with the Indians. In 1704 Baker had been captured by the Indians in the famous Deerfield raid and with the other captives was forced to march to Canada. During this forced march, Baker saw many of his fellow captives die or be killed because they could not keep up with the rest of the group. Baker was eventually able to escape and return to Massachusetts. However, his experiences and suffering caused him to seek the revenge that he achieved in the massacre near Plymouth.

## BALD CAP                                    Elevation 3,090
There are three peaks with rocky ledges in the Mahoosucs—Bald Cap, North Bald Cap and Bald Cap Peak. These peaks were named by E. B. Cook and other members of his family. (See Cook Path.)

## BARNES FIELD
The Barnes Field campground is located about one-half mile farther up the Dolly Copp road beyond the Dolly Copp Campground. The Barnes family built their farm here in the mid 1800's.

## BARTLETT MT.                                Elevation 2,661
## Bartlett, Town of
The town of Bartlett in the Saco River Valley has been described as "an ellipse of fertile land; a river murmuring unseen; a wall of mountains, with Kearsarge looking up and Carrigain looking down the intervale." The town was granted to William Stark and Vere Royce about 1770 after the French and Indian War. However, neither Stark nor Royce ever settled and claimed the town. In 1790 the town was incorporated as Bartlett in honor of Josiah Bartlett, the first American governor of New Hampshire and a signer of the Declaration of Independence just beneath the signature of John Hancock, President of the Continental Congress.

Mt. Bartlett, also named after Josiah Bartlett, is east of Intervale, north of North Conway.

## BASIN, THE

"The Basin" is a large geologic pothole carved in the stream bed of the Pemigewasset River south of Franconia Notch. This pothole has been formed by the swirling action of the sand that is being carried in the rushing waters. When this erosion first started, there existed only a small and insignificant crack in the rock. Over the estimated 25,000 years that it has taken to create this formation, the pothole has grown to a depth of 15 feet and between 30 and 40 feet in diameter.

Pemigewasset, meaning "Rapidly Moving," is the Abenaki name for this river.

## BEECHER CASCADE (Beecher's Cascades)

These waterfalls are found on Crawford Brook to the west of Crawford Notch. The Rev. Henry Ward Beecher, an abolitionist preacher from Brooklyn, New York, visited the White Mountains for many summers between 1872 and 1889. During these long visits Beecher stayed at the Twin Mountain House, where he had a tent and would give sermons each Sunday. Beecher's sister, Harriet Beecher Stowe, the author of *Uncle Tom's Cabin*, accompanied her brother during these visits.

The original name for these waterfalls, "Beecher's Cascades," referred to the series of waterfalls found here. Today's name, Beecher Cascade, in the singular, refers to only one waterfall.

*Tent used by Henry Ward Beecher at Twin Mountain.*
Stereoscopic photo. New Hampshire Historical Society Collection.

Visitors willing to take a short walk may go up the Avalon Trail to these falls.

## BEMIS RIDGE and Mt. Bemis               Elevation 3,705

The Bemis Ridge extends south of Mt. Crawford and is named after Dr. Samuel Bemis, a Boston dentist who spent many summers here at his summer home which is today an inn called "Notchland" (formerly the Inn Unique), south of Crawford Notch in Crawford Glen. After he retired, Dr. Bemis, known to many local people as the "Lord of the Valley," lived here year round until his death in 1882. It was Bemis who was responsible for naming Mt. Crawford, the Giant's Stairs and Mt. Resolution. Mt. Bemis rises behind the old Bemis home. Just south of the Frankenstein Cliffs is Bemis Brook.

Timothy Dwight, the President of Yale College and a frequent visitor to the area, described it as follows: "Here the mountains assumed the form of an immense amphitheater; elliptical in its figure; from twelve to fifteen miles in length; from two to four in breadth; and crowned with summits of vast height and amazing grandeur."

## BETHLEHEM

Between Franconia and Twin Mountain lies the small town of Bethlehem. This town was originally known as Lloyd's Hill after James Lloyd of Boston to whom the area had been granted in 1773. On Christmas Day 1779 the name was changed to Bethlehem. In 1891 there were more than 16 hotels capable of

*Beecher's Cascades.* 1875 Bierstadt stereoscopic view. From the author's collection.

accommodating over 1,700 guests in Bethlehem. The altitude of the town was particularly attractive to people suffering from hay fever.

In 1882 Samuel Drake described watching the sunsets from Bethlehem as follows:

> From no other village are so many mountains visible at once; at no other has the landscape such length and breadth for giving full effect to these wonderful displays.

## BIGELOW LAWN

The Bigelow Lawn, an alpine garden area between the Lakes of the Clouds and the summit of Mt. Washington, is named in honor of Dr. Jacob Bigelow, a physician and botanist from Boston. Dr. Bigelow and Dr. Francis Boott together researched the alpine areas of the Presidential Range and found plants that were native to Greenland, Siberia, Lapland, and Labrador. One of the grasses found here has been named "Bigelow Sedge."

## BOISE ROCK

Located to the east of Route 93 in Franconia Notch is a large glacial boulder named after Thomas Boise, (also Booise and Boyce), from Woodstock, New Hampshire. In the early 1800's, Boise found shelter under this boulder during a winter storm which made it impossible for him to continue through the Notch with his horse. Boise is said to have killed the horse and then wrapped himself in the skin for protection. When rescuers found Boise, the frozen hide that he was wrapped in had protected him from a certain winter death.

## BOND, MT.                                          Elevation 4,714
Located west of Zealand Notch in the Pemigewasset Wilderness is Mt. Bond, named after Professor G. P. Bond of Harvard University. Bond was an explorer and early map-maker of the White Mountains. To the south of the summit of the mountain are the Bondcliffs.

## BOOTT SPUR
This ridge, south of the summit of Mt. Washington, is named in honor of Dr. Francis Boott, a physician and botanist, who explored the Presidential range in the early 1800's with Dr. Jacob Bigelow.

## BOURNE, LIZZIE
The Lizzie Bourne Monument is located on the northern side of the summit of Mt. Washington near the Cog Railway tracks. Lizzie Bourne, from Kennebunk, Maine, died near this spot in September 1855. She, her uncle and his daughter left the Glen House and intended to spend the night at the summit of the mountain. Near the half-way house workmen met the party and advised them against continuing because of the changing weather. As it became darker and later in the day the weather continued to get worse, and Lizzie Bourne became exhausted from the climb. Exhaustion forced her to lie down and attempt to seek shelter in rocks above the treeline. That evening she died of exposure.

## BOWMAN, MT.                                       Elevation 3,450
Mt. Bowman is located on the Castellated Ridge on the northwestern side of Mt. Jefferson above the town of Randolph.

# BRETTON WOODS

When John Bowman and his son Hiram operated the Bowman Tavern in the early 1800's in the town of Randolph, life there was described as "that of the savage wilderness." US Route 2 and the Boston and Maine Railroad today cross what were once the fields of the Bowman farm. A second source claims that Mt. Bowman was named to honor Selwyn Z. Bowman who had served as an assistant on a mountain survey expedition.

## BRETTON WOODS (See Carroll, Town of)

## BROOK TRAIL
The Brook Trail and the Liberty Trail ascend Mt. Chocorua from Route 113A. When the Liberty Trail was first built by James Liberty in 1887, it was a toll path to the summit of the mountain. In 1892, the footpath was made into a bridle path. The Brook Trail, following along the banks of the Clay Brook, was cut by the local people as a free path to the summit.

## BRYCE PATH
The Bryce Path starts near Echo Lake in North Conway and ascends Cathedral Ledge. This trail was cleared in 1907 by the British Ambassador to the United States, Lord James Bryce. When Bryce first visited the White Mountains in 1870 he stayed at the same inn as Ralph Waldo Emerson and wrote in his journal:

> Nothing can be lovelier than these woods, so much more varied than an Alpine and richer than a British forest. In the evening some talk with Emerson, who discourses in a rather set and continuous way without stiffness however, and using sufficiently simple and natural language.

## BUMPUS BASIN and Bumpus Brook

Bumpus Basin is located on the northern side of the Howker Ridge on the northeastern side of Mt. Madison. Bumpus Brook runs through this basin. The Bumpus family were early settlers in the Town of Randolph. In 1824, when Randolph was incorporated, Silas Bumpus was the Town Clerk.

## BURT RAVINE

Burt Ravine is located on the western side of Mt. Washington. The Cog Railway passes through this ravine in its ascent and descent of the mountain.

In 1901 this ravine was named in honor of Henry M. Burt who in 1877 started the publication of *Among the Clouds*, the only newspaper that has ever been printed on the summit of a mountain. The newspaper ceased publication in 1917.

## CABOT, MT.　　　Elevation 1,503

Located above the Philbrook Farm Inn in Shelburne, Mt. Cabot is named after an early guest, Edward Cabot of Boston.

## CANNON MOUNTAIN (Profile Mountain)　　　Elevation 4,077

Cannon Mountain, also known as Profile Mountain, is located in Franconia Notch across from Mt. Lafayette. This mountain is named after the oblong rock near its summit that has the appearance of a cannon. (Some early maps show this as Freak Mountain.) There are knobs on the Kinsman Ridge, south of Cannon Mountain, that are called the "cannon balls."

The "Old Man of the Mountain" profile is a part of this mountain. (See Franconia)

### CARLO COL and Carlo Mt.　　　Elevation 3,562

Located in the Mahoosuc Range north of Shelburne, this col and mountain are said to be named after a dog at the Philbrook Farm Inn in Shelburne. The dog was the pet and companion of E. B. Cook who vacationed in both Shelburne and Randolph. (See Cook Path.)

### CARRIGAIN, MT.　　　Elevation 4,678

Mt. Carrigain is named after Philip Carrigain of Concord, New Hampshire. Carrigain was born in Concord in 1772 and died there in 1842. He was a graduate of Dartmouth College and became the N. H. Secretary of State between 1805 and 1810. In 1816 he published what was then the most complete map of New Hampshire. However, that map did not identify Mt. Washington, which had been known by that name since 1784.

### CARROLL, TOWN OF

The town of Carroll, east of Bethlehem, was granted in 1772 to a group of Englishmen and was first known as "Bretton Woods." One of these Englishmen was Sir Thomas Wentworth who lived at "Bretton Hall" in Yorkshire. Hence the name Bretton Woods here in the White Mountains. (Sir Thomas Wentworth was a cousin of Governor John Wentworth of New Hampshire.) It has also been suggested that this name is a reference to the 1745 English victory over the French on Cape Breton Island.

The town's name was changed in 1832 to "Carroll" after Charles Carroll of Maryland, a signer of the Declaration of Independence and friend of the Governor of New Hampshire.

Carroll visited the White Mountains on his way to Canada in 1776 to discuss a possible merger between the United States and Canada. Carroll died in 1832, the same year that the town was named after him.

During the last half of the 19th century this town had numerous summer hotels which, with the exception of the Mount Washington Hotel at Bretton Woods, are gone today. Today, the town of Carroll includes the places known as Twin Mountain, Fabyan, Marshfield and Bretton Woods.

## CARTER RANGE

This range, including Carter Dome and Carter Notch extends south from Gorham on the eastern side of Route 16. There are two stories about who "Carter" was. Sweetser's guide describes a legend about two hunters named Carter and Hight who worked together in these mountains. (See Mt. Hight.)

One story simply says that Carter was a hunter in these mountains. Visitors are therefore left to imagine the wanderings of a lone hunter among the hills.

A second account states that this range is named for a Concord, New Hampshire physician, Dr. Ezra Carter, who was an early botanist and explored this area in search of herbs and roots to use in his medicines.

## CASTELLATED RIDGE and Castle Trail

The Castellated Ridge is located on the northwestern side of Mt. Jefferson and is visible from Route 2 in Randolph.

This ridge is named for the rock ledges that, from a distance, appear to resemble the ruins of castles and forts. Drake de-

scribed this ridge as, "a sloping ridge of brown granite, broken at its summit into a long line of picturesque towers and battlements." The Castle Trail, which ascends this ridge, was cut between 1883 and 1884 by E. B. Cook, George Sargent, Laban Watson, Albert Mathews, and Hubbard Hunt. (Cook, Sargent and Watson were active elsewhere in the White Mountains and are discussed below. Hunt was a resident of Randolph and did much work for the AMC in building and maintaining trails. The author has no additional information about Albert Mathews.)

## CENTENNIAL TRAIL

The Centennial Trail, cleared in 1976 by the AMC, ascends Mt. Hayes in the Mahoosuc Range from the North Road in Shelburne, New Hampshire.

The AMC was celebrating its Centennial year when this trail from the North Road to the Mahoosuc trail was relocated.

## CHAMPNEY FALLS and Champney Falls Trail

This waterfall, on Mt. Chocorua, and the trail that leads to it are named in honor of Benjamin Champney, an artist who came to North Conway for many years to paint views of the mountains. (See Conway.)

## CHANDLER RIDGE , Chandler Brook, and Chandler Brook Trail

The Auto Road up Mt. Washington passes over the Chandler Ridge, named after Benjamin Chandler. On August 7, 1856, at the age of 75, Chandler became lost while hiking on this ridge.

---

*The Castellated Ridge.* Samuel A. Drake.
From the author's collection.

Rescuers were unsuccessful in their search efforts, and Chandler's body was not found until the following year. The Chandler Brook and the Chandler Brook Trail ascend the ridge from the Great Gulf.

## CHERRY MOUNTAIN                    Elevation 3,554

Cherry Mountain is located east of Route 115 in the town of Jefferson. Several trails go to the summit.

A state historic marker along the road indicates the site of the July 10, 1885 Cherry Mountain Slide. At that time, an estimated one million tons of trees, mud, and boulders fell from the mountain. Dan Walker, a workman at the Oscar Stanley farm, died from injuries that he received from the slide. The home, barn, and cattle were all lost.

After the slide many people visiting at the area hotels came over to view the devastation. A small restaurant was here to provide food for these visitors. Today nature has healed the scars left by this disaster.

## CHOCORUA, MT.                    Elevation 3,475

Mt. Chocorua is located in the Sandwich Range to the west of the town of Conway. Many trails ascend the summit from different directions.

The physical prominence of Mt. Chocorua is undeniable. Darby Field referred to this mountain as a "striking sentinel" as he found his way to Mount Washington in 1642. Another writer has described Chocorua as "a true alp, brave, aloof, titanic with

---

*Peak of Chocorua.* Photo by Eugene S. Jones.
New Hampshire Historical Society Collection.

a lonely beauty." Whenever Starr King wrote about Chocorua
he appears to have used a different adjective including: defiant,
jagged, gaunt and grisly, tired, haggard, desolate, ghostly, crouch-
ing, gallant, steel-hooded, rugged, torn and lonely, craggy,
proud and haughty. Another 19th century hiker and writer
described Chocorua as "most individual" with its "ashen spire
and olive green flanks."

Chocorua is named after Chief Chocorua of the Pequawket
Indians. Chief Chocorua, described as a silent haughty warrior
with a brooding passion in his eyes, remained in the White
Mountains after the rest of his tribe had fled to Canada from
New Hampshire following the Dover Raid of 1686. After time
had passed, Chief Chocorua made a trip to Canada to visit his
tribe, but he left his son with the Cornelius Campbell family.
While Chocorua was away, his son accidentally swallowed
poison and died. Upon learning of this death when he returned,
Chocorua blamed the Campbell family for the death of his son
and killed Caroline Campbell and her children. Cornelius
Campbell pursued the Chief up the mountain and demanded
that Chocorua surrender, to which the Chief angrily responded:
"The Great Spirit gave life to Chocorua and Chocorua will not
throw it away at the command of a white man!" Chocorua then
shouted a curse on the white settlers:

> May the Great Spirit curse you when he speaks in the
> clouds and his words are fire! Lightning blast your
> crops! Wind and fire destroy your homes! The Evil
> One breathe death on your cattle! Panthers howl and
> wolves fatten on your bones!

Then Chocorua leapt from the cliff to his death as Campbell
fired his musket.

Future settlers attributed the wolf and bear raids and the death of their cattle to this Indian curse. The death of cattle in the town of Jackson was discovered to be due to concentrations of lime in the water rather than Chocorua's legendary curse.

## CHURCH PATH

This short path on Randolph Hill goes from the Randolph Hill Road to the Randolph Church on Route 2. It was cleared by the Torrey family. The Rev. Joseph Torrey, his wife and their sons visited Randolph regularly beginning in 1878. At that time visitors arrived in the White Mountains by train and stayed for several months. As all of these visitors had no readily available means of transportation, they often turned to building paths. In order to get to the guest house where they stayed, the family first cleared what would become known as the Torrey Path, (now abandoned), from the railway station up to Randolph Hill. Later they cleared other trails in Randolph including the Diagonal, the Church Path and the Pasture Path. On Mts. Madison and Adams, the Torrey family cleared the Spur Trail and the Howker Ridge Trail.

## CLAY, MT.                                              Elevation 5,532

Mt. Clay, named by William Oakes in honor of the American statesman Henry Clay, is located between Mt. Washington and Mt. Jefferson. (See Presidential Range.)

## CLEVELAND, MT.                                         Elevation 2,397

Mt. Cleveland, once known as Round Mountain, is located northwest of Route 3 between Franconia and Twin Mountain. This mountain is named for President Grover Cleveland who

summered in Tamworth, New Hampshire. During his two non-consecutive terms as president, over 26 million acres of forest reserves were created throughout the country that were later to become national forests.

### CLINTON, MT. (Mt. Pierce)                Elevation 4,312

Located south of Mt. Washington in the southern peaks and just north of Mt. Jackson, this mountain is named after DeWitt Clinton, the promoter of the Erie Canal, Mayor of New York, U. S. Senator and Governor of New York.

In 1903, the New Hampshire legislature changed the name to Mt. Pierce to honor President Franklin Pierce who was from New Hampshire. Both names, Clinton and Pierce, are still used today. Depending upon the map that is being used either Clinton or Pierce is shown parenthetically. The Mt. Clinton Road crosses from Crawford Notch to Marshfield below the summit of this mountain. Without a Mt. Clinton, there would be no Mt. Clinton Road. (There has never been a "Mt. Pierce Road.")

Abel Crawford was known to have called this "Bald Hill."

### COG RAILWAY

The three mile Cog Railway ascends the western side of Mt. Washington from the Base Station at Marshfield in the town of Carroll.

The idea for the railroad originated with Sylvester Marsh, a native of Campton, New Hampshire, who later moved to

*Base Station, Mount Washington.* Boston & Maine train unloading passengers onto the Cog Railway. Photo by Eugene S. Jones. New Hampshire Historical Society Collection.

Littleton and was described as a "mild mannered lunatic." Marsh had invented meat packing machinery and had made his fortune in the mid-west. In planning the railroad, Marsh adopted the cog system that had been invented by Herrick Aiken and his son Walter Aiken of Franklin, New Hampshire.

As he was building a railroad, Marsh needed to obtain a charter from the New Hampshire legislature. The idea for a railway up Mt. Washington was considered with more amusement than serious thought by the legislature and the charter was quickly granted. It is said that one of the legislators offered an amendment authorizing Marsh to extend his railroad to the moon.

The railway company was formed in 1865 as the Mt. Washington Steam Railway Company. In 1866 construction began and an engine, to become known as *Old Peppersass*, was demonstrated for the first time. Three years after construction had begun the first trip to the summit of the mountain was made on July 3, 1869.

Chisholm's guide book described the Cog as follows: "The locomotives are queer looking pieces of machinery, chunky and ungainly but of enormous power." In ascending and descending from Mt. Washington, the engine pushes the passenger car which is never coupled to the engine during the trip. After the first ¼ mile, the trip is entirely built on a trestle ranging from two feet to 30 feet off the ground. The most famous section is "Jacob's Ladder," where the track is 30 feet above the ground.

The name "Jacob's Ladder" first referred to the steepest

*Jacob's Ladder, Cog Railway.* Photo by Eugene S. Jones. New Hampshire Historical Society Collection.

section of the Fabyan Path, a now abandoned footpath to the summit of Washington. That trail was described by Eastman as "the nearest approach to the perpendicular which the conscience of a mountaineer will permit." When the Cog Railway was built, the title "Jacob's Ladder" was transferred to the new trestle, the steepest grade of the railway.

After the construction of the railway, Marsh lost control of his company to the Aiken family. Walter Aiken later built the Mt. Washington Summit House, a hotel at the top of the mountain.

In 1929, *Old Peppersass* was brought out of retirement to make a historical 60th Anniversary trip. Despite comments from some worried engineers, the engine was taken up the mountain. Above Jacob's Ladder the engine failed and the train rolled backwards and crashed into Burt Ravine. *Old Peppersass* was recovered and reassembled as an historic attraction at the Base Station.

In 1967 eight people were killed and many were injured in a second accident. An investigation of that accident found that a switch had either been improperly set or that it had been tampered with by an unknown person. No mechanical error was found to have contributed to that accident.

The Cog Railway has never been noted for its speed in either ascending or descending the mountain. However, workmen on the railway conceived of a very fast method of going down the tracks on a contraption referred to as a "slideboard" or "Devil's shingle." These boards were approximately three feet long and

*Slideboards on the Cog Railway.* Stereoscopic picture.
New Hampshire Historical Society Collection.

fit over the cog rail. They were equipped with hand controlled friction brakes that the riders supposedly used to control their descent. The average time down the mountain was about ten minutes, but the record time was reported to be two minutes and forty-five seconds.

One story relates how a visitor to the Cog asked how long it takes to get down the mountain. The railway employee replied: "I can't tell exactly, but I stood at the door of the Summit House one day with my watch in one hand and the telephone in the other, and as the fellow let go the brake and started down I hollered in the phone, 'He's off!' and the operator at the Base called back, 'He's here.'" After one railway employee was killed using a slideboard, their use was forbidden. After this, two men from Boston obtained a slideboard and headed down the mountain as a thrill. They were both killed in an accident.

## CONNECTICUT RIVER

Much of the White Mountains lie in the Connecticut River watershed This river, with its headwaters in the Connecticut Lakes in Pittsburg, New Hampshire, is surrounded by green hillsides and fertile valley farms and is the state line between Vermont and New Hampshire. The Native American name for this river was "Quinnehtukgut" or "Long River."

During the early settlement of northern New Hampshire, this river was the only "highway" of either communication or transportation between the new settlements of northern New England and the established towns of southern New England. For this reason all of the early settlements were along the river. The town of Lancaster was settled in 1764 followed by the settling of other northern towns. The earliest means of transportation were the canoes that were hewn from the virgin pines and used on the river. The development of the railroad allowed other towns to develop independently of the river, and it subsequently became of less importance as a highway to the region.

Today the river provides many recreational opportunities including boating, fishing, and swimming.

## CONWAY

Conway and North Conway, settled in 1764 by settlers from Durham and Lee, New Hampshire, have long been a gateway to the White Mountains. The town was named after an Englishman, Henry Seymour Conway.

The area was known as the Pequawket or "Clear Valley Lands Bordering a Crooked River" by the local Indians. This is a reference to the Intervale in North Conway and the Saco River. Pequawket became "Pigwacket" to the early settlers, but this name was soon abandoned. A sulfur spring in the area was popular for a period and caused the area to be known as the "Saratoga of the Mountains."

North Conway was to become a summer colony for artists and one early guide book noted that North Conway "almost owes its existence to artists, who find here the most lovely scenery to transfer to canvas." Chisholm's guidebook reads, "No rural resort in New England has such devoted partisans and ardent admirers, no village in the mountain region has refreshed and renewed so many thousands of weary citizens."

The first known instance of artists making North Conway a base for their work comes from Samuel Thompson who opened his home to artists needing a place to stay. Before this, Thompson's home had been used as an inn by teamsters traveling with their commerce. The work of Thomas Cole in 1827 attracted others to northern New Hampshire. The first artist "colony" was not established until 1850 when Benjamin Champney and John F. Kensett worked in North Conway. By 1856, so many artists were visiting the area that Champney is said to have remarked "Conway...threatens to become almost fashionable." Often during the summer months, fields were said to be dotted with artists, their umbrellas and their canvasses. This was captured by Winslow Homer in his painting, *Artists Sketching in the White Mountains*.

One of the most frequently painted scenes was the intervale, just north of North Conway, now very specifically known as Intervale. Today the view from the parking area here is just as it was in the middle of the last century because it is in a flood plain where no development can occur. From here the mountains served as a backdrop for the fields and lower hills that surrounded the artists.

The White Mountain artists were most active in the middle of the 19th century. After the Civil War photographs became available and were less expensive than paintings and drawings. In addition, by the late 19th century and into the early 20th century, the logging industry was stripping the hills of their forests. This logging spoiled the views of the mountains and drove the artists away.

While most of the artists painted the scenery that surrounded them, the work of Winslow Homer is noted for how it recorded what the "tourists" were doing during their visits. Homer's work not only captured the artists painting the countryside, but other daily activities. There are two Homer paintings showing riders on the bridle path. In one of these, *The Bridle Path—Mt. Washington*, there is a group of riders with several men in the forefront of the picture. It is said that one of these men is Homer himself. A second painting, *Mt. Washington*, depicts a solitary blond girl riding a white horse up the bridle path.

Some of the "White Mountain art" was painted by artists who never visited the area but copied the works of others. William Henry Bartlett produced numerous engravings for *American Scenery*, published in England. The *View of Meredith*, painted by E. C. Coates in 1851, is a copy of one of Bartlett's prints published in 1838. Coates is never known to have visited New Hampshire. *The Notch House, White Mountains*, depicting Crawford Notch, was another of Bartlett's 1838 prints (see page 56). At a later date, the original plate was used when the print was re-issued, but the printer omitted Bartlett's name and changed the style of the lettering in the title. In 1857, Currier and Ives copied Bartlett's print when they printed *The Notch House, White Mountain*. The Currier and Ives print is noted for the missing "s" in "Mountain" and for the fact that the building that was depicted had been destroyed by fire three years earlier.

Today, artists continue to visit and paint the scenery in the White Mountains.

## COOK PATH

Eugene Beauharnais Cook was a 19th century path builder in Randolph, where, after his first visit in 1878, he continued to summer at the Ravine House for many years. The Cook Path from the Randolph Hill Road to the Ice Gulch honors the work that Cook did in opening up the woods. Cook was often accompanied by his sister, Mrs. Lucia Pychowska, and her daughter, Miss Marian Pychowska, who contributed articles of their own to the AMC publication, *Appalachia*.

In 1884 Cook and George A. Sargent completed what was then a record 20½ hour hike. Starting from the Ravine House in Randolph, they first climbed to Mt. Washington. They then continued down the Crawford Path to Crawford Notch and returned to Randolph through the town of Jefferson.

## COOS COUNTY

Coos County, the northernmost county in New Hampshire, was established in 1803. Some sources say that "Coos" means "pines" and is therefore a reference to the evergreen forest that covers the region. Some of the Native Americans who had lived here had been known as the "Coo-ash-aukes," or "Dwellers in the Place of the Pines." Other sources say that Coos is the Abenaki word "chou" meaning "crooked." This is a reference to the bend in the Connecticut River that forms the western border of the county with the State of Vermont. Earlier, the "Coos area" extended to Haverhill, New Hampshire, known then as the "Lower Coos." The "Upper Coos" began at Lancaster and included the entire northern part of the state. Different descriptions of the area published between 1784 and the middle of the 19th century spell "Coos" any of five ways: Coos, Cohos, Cowass, Koes, and Cohofs.

It was not until 1842 that Pittsburg, the northernmost town in the county, was determined to be a part of New Hampshire and the United States rather than Canada. For a period of time

Pittsburg had been known as the Indian Stream Republic and as a "republic" had printed its own money and raised a militia.

## COOSAUKE FALLS

The Coosauke Falls are located on the Bumpus Brook on the northern side of Mt. Madison. These falls were named by William H. Peek, a summer resident of Randolph. Peek adopted two Abenaki words to name these falls. However, he was mistaken in the meaning that he thought the new name would have. Peek thought that "Coos" meant "rough" and that the name signified "Rough Place." Perhaps a more correct meaning would be "Place of Pines."

## COPP, DOLLY (Campground)

Today, the Dolly Copp Campground occupies the land that was farmed by the Copp family in the 1800's. Hayes Copp made his farm here in Martins Grant, (originally granted to Thomas Martin of Portsmouth, New Hampshire, after the French and Indian War), in 1826 and married Dolly Emery of Jackson, New Hampshire, in 1831. When Copp purchased his land he had no money. Over time, he paid for it with the wheat, barley, and oats that he grew on his farm. After her wedding, Dolly rode the horse that her father had given her, pulling her personal and household goods to her new home. After a short period, Hayes Copp replaced his log cabin with a frame house. For the next 50 years the Copp family lived on this farm and greeted the many stages and tourists that stopped to visit with them as they passed the farm on their way to the Glen House and Mt. Washington.

It might be said that Dolly Copp had one of the earliest "road-side stands" and "craft shops" in the White Mountains.

The early writings of King and Drake encouraged the tourists to request that the stages stop at the Copp farm on the way to the Glen House. Dolly sold the visiting tourists many homemade products including apple-butter, (using her butter and the apples from her small orchard), cheese, candles, maple syrup and linen. In addition to being an early "craft shop," the farm served as an inn between Jackson and Randolph. It has been said that Dolly charged "a shilling all around"—meaning that she charged 25¢ per meal, 25¢ a bed, and 25¢ for the care of a visitor's horse.

In 1881, after 50 years of marriage, the Copps separated. Dolly Copp moved to her daughter's home in Auburn, Maine, while her husband returned to his native home of Stowe, Maine. The Copp farm was added to the White Mountain National Forest in 1915. The remnants of the farm, stone foundations, and apple trees are the silent reminders of this pioneering family.

For a brief period, Dolly Copp's name was given to "Dolly Copp Ginger Ale" that was bottled in Gorham.

In 1952 Anne Miller Downes published a fictional account of Dolly Copp's life in the book *The Pilgrim Soul*.

The Hayes Copp Cross Country Ski Trail goes from the Dolly Copp Campground to the Great Gulf Trail and then back to the campground.

## COPPERMINE BROOK

As its name suggests, Coppermine Brook, on the western side of Cannon Mountain, is named for the copper mines that

---

*Stagecoach at the Crawford House.* Photo by Willis Boyd Allen. The New Hampshire Historical Society Collection.

existed here prior to the Civil War. Other small copper mines existed elsewhere in the Franconia area.

## CRAG CAMP

Crag Camp, an overnight cabin owned by the Randolph Mountain Club (RMC), is located on a rocky outcrop overlooking King Ravine. The cabin was built by Nelson Smith in 1909 and was given to the RMC in 1939. There are plans to rebuild this cabin in 1993.

Unlike the AMC cabins, hikers must take all of their food with them when they use this or other camps maintained by this club.

## CRAWFORDS

There is perhaps no other single family who made such enormous and legendary contributions to the early settlement of the White Mountains as the Crawfords. They are remembered in Crawford Notch, Mt. Crawford (elevation 3,129), the Crawford Path, Ethan's Pond, the Crawford House site, Mt. Tom, Mt. Davis, the Davis Path, Crawford Brook, and in the many legends that have been included in Lucy Crawford's *History of the White Mountains*.

Abel Crawford left the fertile Connecticut River valley farm in Guildhall, Vermont, for the hills of New Hampshire and became the first settler in the valley west of Mt. Washington. For having spent a winter in the notch, providing services for the travelers, Abel Crawford was deeded 100 acres near the site of the present Fabyan Railway Station. His first cabin, built in

*Abel Crawford.* Samuel A. Drake.
From the author's collection.

1791, was sold to his father-in-law Eleazar Rosebrook, after Rosebrook had visited the area. At that time, Abel Crawford moved his family further into the valley. Lucy Crawford was to write that Abel Crawford had moved to this isolated area because he was "ambitious, enterprising and public spirited." She believed that Abel had an early goal of building a road through what was then known as the "Great Notch" to better serve the residents of the Connecticut River valley.

Crawford's most famous son was Ethan Allen Crawford, born in 1792. Ethan Allen Crawford left New Hampshire in 1811, served in the military and settled in New York state, not planning to return to New Hampshire. When his grandfather, Eleazar Rosebrook, was very ill and needed assistance on his farm, Ethan Allen Crawford returned to the White Mountains and soon after married his first cousin, Lucy. After the death of his grandfather, Ethan Allen Crawford took over the farm and inn. Ethan's home and inn, the "Old Moosehorn Tavern," burned in 1818, but he rebuilt it.

By this time, Ethan's father, Abel had settled in Notchland and had a small inn there for overnight guests. This inn came to be called the Mt. Crawford House.

In 1828 the "Notch House," later the site of the Crawford House, was built by Abel Crawford and his son Ethan Allen. This inn was managed by Ethan's brother, Thomas. At this time the Crawfords became the first family with a chain of hotels in northern New Hampshire—three hotels within a twelve mile distance.

In 1837 Ethan Allen Crawford sold his inn. It would later be

*Crawford House.* J. S. Conant from Howard & Crocker, *A History of New England.* From the author's collection.

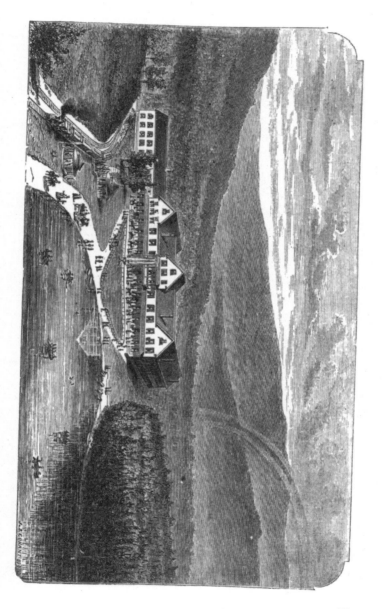

destroyed by fire in 1854, as was a new inn in 1859. Nathaniel Hawthorne once described Ethan's hotel as "at once the pleasure house of fashionable tourists and the homely inn of country travelers." The inn in Crawford Notch hosted American Presidents, Pierce, Grant, Hayes, Garfield and Harding during their respective visits to the White Mountains. The last "Crawford House" hotel in Crawford Notch closed in 1975 and was destroyed by fire in November 1977.

Ethan Allen Crawford became a legend in his own lifetime. He stood 6' 3", possessed enormous strength, and many accounts described him as the "Giant of the Mountain." In 1819, with his father Abel, Ethan built the first path to the summit of Mt. Washington. In 1821 Ethan Allen Crawford built the first structure on the summit of Mt. Washington to provide shelter for the guests that he guided up there. Thomas Crawford later improved and widened the foot path to be a bridle path for horses. When the Bridle Path was completed in 1840, Abel Crawford, at the age of 75, became the first person to ride a horse to the summit of Mt. Washington. With the opening of the Bridle Path many more White Mountain visitors were able to reach the summit of Mt. Washington. The horses and the Bridle Path are immortalized in Winslow Homer's painting, *The Bridle Path*. The Rev. Henry Ward Beecher described a ride along the Bridle Path as follows:

> As I rode along this jagged and broken path, except of my horse's feet, there was not a single sound. There was no wind. There was nothing for it to sing through if there had been ever so much. There were no birds. There were no chirping insects.... There was perfect peace, perfect stillness, universal brightness, the fullness of vision, and a wondrous glory in the heaven and

all over the earth. The earth was to me as it were unpeopled. I saw neither towns nor cities, neither houses nor villages, neither smoke nor motion nor sign of life. I stopped and imagined that I was as they who first explored this ridgy wilderness, and knew that as far as eye could reach not a white man lived.

An early guidebook noted that not all visitors went by horse: "Sometimes the ascent is made on foot, but on account of the unparalleled roughness and steepness of these mountain paths, this method (walking) is to most persons too wearisome for enjoyment."

With the opening of the Cog Railway, the use of horses on the Bridle Path became obsolete and the trail permanently became a hikers trail, known today as the Crawford Path. Today that path, part of the Appalachian Trail, crosses Mt. Clinton (Pierce), Mt. Eisenhower (Pleasant), Mt. Franklin, Mt. Monroe, passes by the Lakes of the Clouds and then ascends Mt. Washington.

Ethan Allen Crawford was a hotel proprietor, a legendary guide and a trapper and hunter of bear, moose, deer, wolves, otter, sable and lynx. One story of Crawford's hunting exploits has been described by Sweetser:

> Many years ago, when Ethan Allen Crawford was ranging in the woods, he encamped on these shores for a night. While catching trout for supper, he saw two large brown moose among the lily-pads, and by quick action he succeeded in killing them both. After a glorious feast of trout and moose-meat, he retired to sleep between the skins of the fallen animals, regardless of the wolves that were howling on every side. Since that night, the pond has been known as Ethan's Pond.

In her history of the White Mountains, Lucy Crawford recounts how Ethan Allen Crawford "made considerable havoc

among the wild animals" and a "handsome profit from them." But in his later years, Crawford was to note, "There used to be great quantities of fur taken round these mountains; but wild animals have all been hunted so much, they are getting to be scared."

The Crawfords kept some wild animals at their farm as entertainment for visitors. Lucy Crawford was to write:

> These animals were of no use to us, they were an expense; but I always liked to have such things to show our friends and visitors as they all seemed to be delighted in viewing them.

Ethan and Lucy Crawford were always in financial trouble despite their best efforts at running their inn and small farm. At one time Crawford's creditors had him jailed in Lancaster. After the August 1826 storm that destroyed the Willey farm and killed that entire family, the Crawford farm was also left devastated— fences and crops were destroyed. In 1837, in poor health and after losing their property to their creditors, Ethan and Lucy Crawford moved to Guildhall, Vermont. Not happy there, the Crawfords returned to the White Mountains in 1843 and rented a hotel near their old one. Ethan Allen Crawford, the "Giant of the Hills," died three years later on June 22, 1846, at the age of 54. Ethan's father, Abel Crawford, "The Patriarch of the Mountains," died five years later in 1851 at the age of 85. Lucy Crawford survived her husband for 23 years and died on February 17, 1869.

In 1846 "Lucy, Wife of Ethan Allen Crawford, Esq." published *The History of the White Mountains from the First*

---

*The Notch in the Mountains, White Mountains.* W. H. Bartlett. From the author's collection.

CRAWFORDS

*Settlement of Upper Coos and Pequaket*, based on the diary that she had kept during her years in the White Mountains. This classic history has been republished and is today available from the AMC.

There is no other single 19th century family that contributed so much to the opening up of the White Mountains. The thousands of guests who visited the growing number of hotels during the latter half of the 19th century and today's visitors, as they rush through in their cars and motor homes, owe much to the vision and fortitude of the Crawford family who struggled here for so long and with so little reward.

The discovery of "Crawford Notch" was made by Timothy Nash in 1771, reportedly as he was hunting a moose and exploring what would become known as Mt. Mitten. Nash was a Lancaster area hunter who received a grant of land, known as Nash and Sawyer Location, as a reward for finding the notch. Nash and his friend Benjamin Sawyer received this after they satisfactorily proved that the notch existed by bringing a horse through it. In 1803, the New Hampshire legislature chartered a turnpike to be built through what was then known by three names: "Notch of the Mountain," "White Mountain Notch" and "The Great Notch."

In this notch is Saco Lake, the headwaters of the Saco River, Saco being the Abenaki word for "flowing out" or "outlet." Today, the Saco River flows through a pipe as it goes through the notch. This was made necessary when the railroad was built and the road was widened. Not far from Saco Lake are streams that are tributaries to both the Ammonoosuc and the Connecticut Rivers. The Crawford House hotel was at the highest point in the notch. The roof of the hotel constituted a "divide" between two watersheds as the rain on one side drained into the Saco River and flowed out to the Atlantic Ocean through Saco, Maine, south of Portland. Rain on the other side of the hotel roof drained to the west and into the Connecticut River and finally into Long Island Sound at Old Lyme, Connecticut.

Nathaniel Hawthorne described Crawford Notch as "a great artery through which the lifeblood of internal commerce is continually throbbing between Maine and the Green Mountains and the shores of the St. Lawrence." It has been reported that the first article of "commerce" that was brought through the notch was a barrel of rum, taken to the Whipple farm in Jefferson.

## CRESCENT, MT. Elevation 3,230

Named for its "crescent shape," Mt. Crescent stands above Randolph Hill, to the north of Route 2. The Ice Gulch is on the eastern side of this mountain. For many years the Mt. Crescent House, a summer hotel, stood at the base of this mountain.

## CULHANE BROOK

Culhane Brook flows off the eastern side of Mt. Madison and through the Dolly Copp Campground. The Culhane family was one of the three early families in this area, the others being the Copps and the Barnes.

## CUTLER RIVER

The Cutler River flows out of Tuckerman Ravine on the eastern side of Mt. Washington. Hikers will cross this river as they hike into that area. The stream is named in honor of the Reverend Manasseh Cutler, a botanist, who in 1784, was a member of the first scientific expedition to Mt. Washington led

CUTTER, LOUIS F.

by Jeremy Belknap. During this expedition Cutler wrongly determined the elevation of Mt. Washington to be 10,000 feet. It was Cutler who first described the alpine vegetation that is found on Mt. Washington—a more lasting contribution than the elevation of the mountain. Cutler returned to Mt. Washington in 1804. Later scientists to continue with his work include, Bigelow, Boott, Oakes and Tuckerman, all of whom have places named after them.

## CUTTER, LOUIS F.

Louis F. Cutter is best remembered in the White Mountains as the "Dean of Maps" for the AMC. Cutter, an 1886 graduate of MIT, spent many summers in Randolph and, like many of the other early trail makers, used the Ravine House as his headquarters. Cutter's primary work, begun in 1883, became the 1886 map of the Mt. Washington Range. It is still today the basis for the maps that are sold by the AMC, included in the AMC *White Mountain Guide*, and used by hikers. The 1886 map has subsequently been improved by including U. S. Geological Survey information and the trails of the Appalachian Mountain Club, the Randolph Mountain Club, and the U. S. Forest Service.

In 1988, the Boston Museum of Science and the AMC jointly published a map of Mount Washington and the Presidential Range that had been prepared by Bradford Washburn using modern laser and computer technology.

## DARTMOUTH, MT.                    Elevation 3,721

Located in the town of Jefferson, to the west of the Jefferson Notch Road, Mt. Dartmouth and the Dartmouth Range both

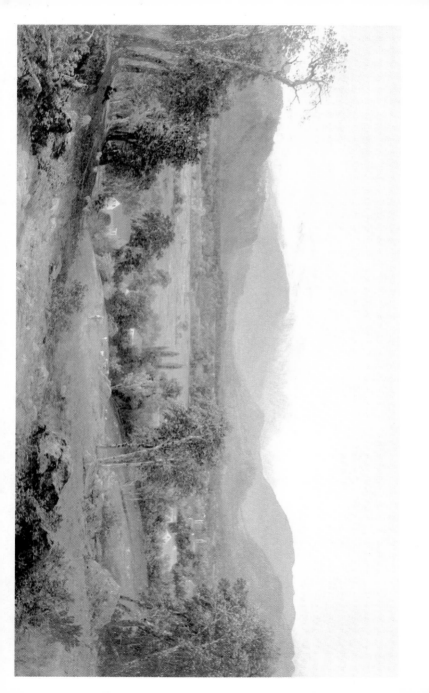

Winslow Homer, *Mt. Washington.*

Thomas Cole, *The Notch of the White Mountains (Crawford Notch)*.

Edward Hill, *Presidential Range from Jefferson Highlands.*

bear the former name of this town. There are no hiking trails in this range.

## DAVIS, MT. and Davis Path            Elevation 3,800

Mt. Davis, on the Montalban Ridge, and the Davis Path up Mt. Crawford, are named in honor of Nathaniel T. P. Davis. Davis was married to Hannah Crawford, the daughter of Abel Crawford. Davis cleared the trail which bears his name about 1845, when he was the proprietor of the Mt. Crawford House.

## DECEPTION, MT.            Elevation 3,658

Mt. Deception stands above and to the north of Bretton Woods and Fabyan. Sweetser has written that its name originated when a group of people climbed it mistakenly thinking that it was Mt. Washington. Today there are no trails on this mountain.

## DEVIL'S DEN

This is a damp cave, only accessible by ropes, located on the face of Mt. Willard in Crawford Notch. In 1850 Franklin Leavitt of Lancaster was lowered by ropes to look into this cave. He said that he found bones at the opening and then immediately signalled to his friends to help him back up the cliff. Further explorations of the cave found no evidence of any bones.

## DIAGONAL TRAIL

The Diagonal Trail on Randolph Hill goes from the Pasture Path down to the old Ravine House site near Lake Durand. During their visits to Randolph, the Torrey family stayed at what was then known as the "Kelsey Cottage," which became the Mountain View House and is now a private residence. In order to walk quickly down to their friends staying at the Ravine House, the Torreys cleared this trail that diagonally crosses Randolph Hill.

## DODGE, The Joe Dodge Lodge

The Joe Dodge Lodge at the AMC Camp in Pinkham Notch is named after the 20th century builder and manager of the modern AMC hut system. Joe Dodge made his first trip to the White Mountains in 1909. He became the hutmaster in Pinkham Notch in 1922 and manager of the AMC hut system in 1928, in which capacity he served until his retirement in 1959. After his retirement, Dodge continued to be active in the area and was known to many people through his daily weather reports on a local radio station. Dodge reportedly said of the weather, "All weather is good weather, some's just different."

During the Dodge years the number of huts was increased, AMC services were expanded and existing huts were enlarged to meet the needs of the growing number of White Mountain visitors. The AMC hut system that the hiker finds today is the one that Dodge first envisioned and then found the resources to build.

In addition to his work with the AMC, Dodge worked closely with Robert S. Monahan of Dartmouth College to re-open the weather observatory on the summit of Mt. Washington in 1932. When Dartmouth College awarded Dodge an honorary degree in 1955, he was cited as "beyond rescue as a legend of all that is unafraid, friendly, rigorously good and ruggedly expressive in the out-of-doors."

## DURAND RIDGE

The town of Randolph was originally granted to the Durand family of London by King George III. When the town was incorporated the name of Durand was changed to Randolph. Today the Durand name is remembered in both Durand Lake, an artificial lake on the northern side of Route 2, and Durand Ridge on the eastern side of King Ravine. It was the Randolph visitor William H. Peek who reportedly named Durand Ridge.

## EAGLE CLIFF

Eagle Cliff is a spur on Mt. Lafayette to the east of Profile Lake in the Franconia Range. This cliff was named in 1858 by the Reverend Thomas Hill after he discovered an eagle's nest high up in the cliff.

## EAGLE MOUNTAIN                    Elevation 1,615

As its name suggests, this mountain, north of Jackson, is named for eagles that once nested here. In his guidebook, Sweetser wrote that "one of its upper crags was formerly the abode of bold and rapacious eagles."

## EDMANDS COL and Edmands Path

Born in 1850, J. Rayner Edmands graduated from MIT in 1869 and became a Professor at the Harvard Observatory. He made his first trip to the White Mountains in 1868 when he visited the town of Jefferson. He later returned for many more summer visits during which he was active in scientific research and path building. During his visits to Randolph, Edmands was one of the many path builders who stayed at the Ravine House. It has been reported that during one of those summers,

Edmands placed a telescope on the Ravine House porch so that he could show his friends what the moon looked like.

In 1876 Edmands was one of the original founders of the Appalachian Mountain Club. He wrote a number of articles for its publications and served as its President in 1886.

The early path builders preferred the word "path" to the word "trail" because they believed that the Indians had had "trails" and that the Conestoga wagons had followed "trails" to the west. In his path construction work Edmands believed paths should follow the contours of a mountain and not go straight up. He concentrated both his time and the time of the workers that he employed with his own funds on improving and restoring existing paths and the creation of new ones. Some have described the work of Edmands as "boulevards" and noted that they were so "smooth that anyone's mother could walk to the summit of Mt. Washington." Amongst the early path builders, It was not universally agreed how paths should be built. Professor Arthur Stanley Pease, a summer visitor in Randolph, is remembered as saying:

> After this lapse of years, I may be pardoned for recalling that there grew up certain prejudices and factions between the Cook and Edmands schools of thought, by reason of which Mr. Cook's family and friends disdained to walk on the too carefully manicured paths of Mr. Edmands and Mr. Edmands boasted that he had never gone up Mt. Crescent, the Ice Gulch or the Pond of Safety, to visit which he would have to walk on some of the Cook trails—for Mr. Edmands a harrowing experience.

In establishing trails above treeline, most notably the Gulfside Trail, Edmands initiated the use of piles of rocks, cairns, to mark the trails.

Edmands is remembered at both Edmands Col and the Edmands Path. A col is a saddle or ridge between mountains. Edmands Col is located between the summits of Mt. Adams and Mt. Jefferson. For many years there was an emergency shelter located here. However, that shelter has been removed because it become a regularly used overnight shelter rather than one used solely for the emergencies for which it was designed and intended.

The Edmands Path leads from the Mt. Clinton Road to the Crawford Path in the col between Mt. Eisenhower and Mt. Franklin. In the tradition of Edmands, this is a well graded path and provides quick access between the Crawford Ridge and the Mt. Clinton Road. Edmands built this path after he left Randolph because of the extensive logging operations there. The continued use of the many trails cleared by Edmands is a tribute to the success of his work.

In early editions of the AMC publication *Appalachia* there are panoramic views of the White Mountains. Edmands had developed a special topographical camera that was used in creating these views and determining the elevations of the mountains. The AMC also attributed to Edmands the invention of a "convenient pack-saddle for the shoulders of pedestrians." All hikers will know what this refers to.

## EISENHOWER, MT. (Mt. Pleasant)          Elevation 4,761

Mt. Eisenhower, in the southern peaks between Mt. Clinton and Mt. Monroe, was named in 1972 after the 34th President, Dwight D. Eisenhower. Sherman Adams, former Governor of New Hampshire and Assistant to President Eisenhower, worked to accomplish this. This mountain was formerly known as Mt. Pleasant. On a few maps it was shown as "Dome Mountain." On one USGS map it was shown as "Pleasant Dome." Mt. Eisenhower is accessible from the Mt. Clinton Road via the Edmands Path or from the Crawford Path.

Maps continue to show a "Mt. Pleasant Brook" on this mountain. This is a misnomer as there is no longer a mountain of that name.

## ELEPHANT HEAD

As seen from the old Crawford House site, this cliff on the eastern side of Crawford Notch has the appearance of an elephant's head with a trunk emerging from the forest. The gray rocks further help create this illusion. It is possible to climb to the top of this ledge via the Webster-Jackson Trail.

**ETHAN'S POND.** See Crawford.

## EVANS NOTCH

Located to the east of the Carter Range and going from Chatham, New Hampshire, to Gilead, Maine, east of Shelburne, is Evans Notch. This notch was named after Captain John Evans, one of the earliest settlers in Fryeburg, Maine, and later a local guide. He was a guide for Jeremy Belknap when he visited the White Mountains in 1784. Belknap described Evans as being "the most knowledgeable person about Mt. Washington."

## FABYAN

Horace Fabyan was a businessman from Portland, Maine, who in 1837, purchased Ethan Allen Crawford's inn. Fabyan's

*The Flume, Franconia Notch.* Samuel A. Drake. From the author's collection. (Note suspended boulder that was washed out in 1883.)

renamed inn, the Mount Washington Hotel, charged $1.50 per night but was destroyed by fire in 1854. The Fabyan name has become associated with an area in the town of Carroll that was later to become the junction of several railroads. Chisholm's 1880 guide reads strangely: "Let us allow the ancient hostelry to recall those bygone days, when old Eleazar Rosebrook came up here from Massachusetts, in 1792, and implanted tree destroying civilization in this lonely glen." It was Abel Crawford, not his father-in-law Eleazar Rosebrook, who first came to this glen.

The Fabyan House, a large hotel that could accommodate 500 guests, was built here in 1874 by the Boston and Maine Railroad. During the summer season, there was an orchestra that played for the guests. This hotel was destroyed by fire in 1951. (See Giant's Grave.)

**FIELD, MT.**                                        Elevation 4,326

In 1642, Darby Field became the first known person to climb what was then called Agiocochook and is today known as Mt. Washington. This ascent of Washington was 130 years before the American revolution.

Field's reasons for climbing the mountain are unknown. He may have been seeking treasures in the mountains. He may have been attempting to find a route between southern New England and the Canadian fur country. Or, he may have very simply wanted just to climb the mountain that could be seen from near his home in southern New Hampshire. It is known that no treasure was found on the summit. For as Jeremy Belknap wrote of his 1784 expedition, "All ſearches for ſubterranean treaſures in the*f*e mountains have as yet proved fruitle*f*s."

Today Mt. Field, above and to the west of Crawford Notch, remembers this first white man to make his way through the wilderness of New Hampshire to the summit of New England and from there be the first to witness the rivers and ranges, the lakes and summits—the vast horizons that extend from Mt. Washington. Prior to being named in honor of Darby Field, this was known as Mt. Lincoln. In order to avoid confusion with the Mt. Lincoln near Franconia Notch the name was changed to Mt. Field.

## FLUME, THE

The flume is a natural granite gorge four miles south of Franconia Notch at the base of Mt. Liberty. This canyon, with perpendicular walls ranging from 70 to 90 feet in height, between 12 and 20 feet wide and over 800 feet long, was formed by the erosion of a basalt dike, a geologic formation, over many thousands of years. Early lithographic prints of The Flume show a large boulder suspended between the walls. That boulder was washed out during a storm in 1883 (see page 67).

The Flume was discovered in 1808 by a woman known as Aunt Jess, the wife of Dave Guernsey, a farmer who had come to New Hampshire from Ireland. At age 93, Aunt Jess accidentally found this secluded and damp gorge while she was either looking for a lost cow or while she was out fishing. Aunt Jess reportedly lived to be 108.

Today the Flume Visitor Center serves as the entrance to this area. At this center information is available, and the visitor can obtain a ride to the entrance to the gorge.

## FRANCONIA

The Franconia Ridge, about 22 miles southwest of Mt. Washington, is east of Route 3 as one travels through Franconia Notch. The ridge does go above tree line but is very distinct from the Presidential Range from a geological point of view. The different summits along the ridge are Mt. Liberty, Little Haystack, Mt. Lincoln, Mt. Lafayette, and Mt. Garfield.

The most famous feature of the Franconia area is across from the Franconia Ridge, on Cannon or Profile Mountain: the Old Man of the Mountains.

The Old Man of the Mountains was first seen in 1805 by Francis Whitcomb and Luke Brooks, two men who were working on the Notch Road that was then being built. The "profile" is in fact five ledges that give the appearance of a human profile when they are all lined up and viewed from near Profile Lake. That lake has also been referred to as the "Old Man's Wash Bowl" and the "Old Man's Mirror" because of the reflection of the profile in its waters.

In 1916 Colonel Greenleaf, the proprietor of the Profile House located in Franconia Notch, noticed that some of the rocks that form the ledges creating the profile were slipping. At that time a mason was called in to repair the forehead. At the present time the Old Man of the Mountain is held together by rods and turnbuckles. Cracks have been filled with epoxy and special drainage channels drain water away from the ledges. All of the ledges have been sprayed with a sealant to protect the profile. Acid rain may be a future threat to this landmark.

---

*The Old Man of the Mountain.* 1875 Bierstadt stereoscopic view.
From the author's collection.

# FRANCONIA

There are different stories about the Indians and the Old Man of the Mountain. One story related how a group of Indians prayed to the "Old Man" to protect them from the Mohawks who lived to the west. A group of Mohawks attacked and ravaged the local Indians. The Mohawks soon afterwards awoke and saw the profile above them and recognized it as the god Manitou. Fearing for their actions, they fell on their faces as the sky produced thunder and lightening. Manitou sentenced these Mohawks to death, and they turned into the stone boulders that are now found in the valley.

In his 1863 *White Mountain Guide* Edson C. Eastman wrote that the "Old Man of the Mountain" was "doubtless an object of veneration to the aboriginal inhabitants." In Sweetser's 1891 guide, he wrote that it was doubtful that the profile was worshipped by any Indians.

Perhaps the strangest book about the White Mountains is *Christus Judex—A Travellers Tale* by Edward Roth, published in 1864. This book describes a 17th century pilgrimage to view the famous profile. An Italian painter had heard of the human profile and being unable to find any suitable model for his portrait of Christ, he set off on his pilgrimage to New Hampshire. Upon arriving at the profile after a lengthy trip, the Indians told the pilgrims how the Face had been happy before white men had appeared and how the Face had "looked with benign and gracious aspect out over the wild forests where the aborigines chased the deer and slew the savage bear." The Indians noted that with the passage of time the Face had begun

---

*The Frankenstein Trestle.* Moses F. Sweetser, *Views of the White Mountains.* From the author's collection.

to lose its "joyful expression and to assume an appearance of grief." The Indian Chief was fearful that the Face was "becoming sterner and more relentless and our oldest sages affirm that, notwithstanding the efforts made by the Good French Blackrobes (priests) to introduce Christianity among us, this continued change only forebodes the utter annihilation of the Indian race and name and that the day of our doom is fast approaching." The Italian painter remained in Franconia Notch until he had completed his portrait.

Others have written differently of this landmark. Nathaniel Hawthorne suggested that the "Great Stone Face" had a profile similar to Daniel Webster. On the other hand, Daniel Webster wrote:

> Men hang out their signs indicative of their respective trades—Shoemakers hang out a gigantic shoe; jewelers a monster watch; even the dentist hangs out a gold tooth; but up in the Franconia Mountains God Almighty has hung out a Sign to Show that in New England He Makes Men.

The Swedish writer Frederika Bremer said that the profile

> ...resembles an old man in a bad humor and with a night cap on his head, who is looking out from the mountain, half inquisitive.

During the 19th century Franconia Notch and the Old Man of the Mountains were protected by the Profile House, one of the largest and most elaborate hotels in the White Mountains. After that hotel burned in 1923 the owners had to sell the land because of their poor financial situation. The standing virgin lumber in the area was of great value and the lumber companies were eager to acquire the land. A joint effort by the Society for the Protection of

New Hampshire Forests and the State of New Hampshire resulted in the purchase of Franconia Notch and the subsequent creation of the Franconia Notch State Park. It is said that funds to purchase this land were contributed by over 15,000 people.

## FRANKENSTEIN CLIFF and Frankenstein Trestle

The Frankenstein Cliff is located above and to the west of Route 302 just south of Crawford Notch. This name is not a reference to any monster but to an artist who worked in the White Mountains. Born in 1820, Godfrey N. Frankenstein immigrated to the United States in 1831. When the family arrived in America they first went to Ohio where Frankenstein started his painting career as a signpainter in Springfield. With his brother John, also an artist, Godfrey Frankenstein later founded the Cincinnati Academy of Art.

Godfrey Frankenstein first visited the White Mountains in 1847 when he camped in Crawford Notch. In later years, he returned to paint the mountains and visit Dr. Samuel Bemis at his home in Notchland.

The Frankenstein Trestle supports the railroad tracks that pass below the cliffs as the tracks wind up and through Crawford Notch. The construction of the railroad and this trestle was an engineering feat that many tourists wanted to view from the special observation cars that the railroads provided (see page 73).

## FRANKLIN, MT. Elevation 5,004

Located southwest of Mt. Washington, between Mt. Monroe and Mt. Eisenhower, is Mt. Franklin named after Benjamin Franklin. This mountain was named in 1820 when a group from Lancaster, New Hampshire climbed Mt. Washington with the purpose of naming all of the mountains. In 1820 there had only been four presidents, so Franklin's name was selected for one of the mountains. The Crawford Path crosses over this mountain.

## GARFIELD, MT. Elevation 4,488

Located at the northern end of the Franconia Ridge, Mt. Garfield was named for President James Garfield after his assassination. It was formerly known as Little Haystack. Garfield Pond, formerly Haystack Lake, is at the base of this mountain.

## GEOLOGY AND GLACIERS

New Hampshire's White Mountains are old mountains when compared with some of the other mountain ranges of the world. Their geologic history begins with an ancient and shallow sea between 350 and 400 million years ago. At that time in the earth's history what we call today the Presidential Range was the bottom of the shallow sea where sediments from volcanic islands were collecting. Over many millions of years these sedimentary deposits were transformed by the earth's heat and the intrusion of molten rock into the granite, or more geologically correct, the mica schist that is found today. The lands were lifted up to their present height by other geologic forces. The summit areas of the Presidential Range have been geologically referred to as the "Presidential Upland" after these now pre-historic and forgotten hills that existed beside a similarly forgotten sea.

Geologically speaking, it is the work of the glaciers that has

---

*Mt. Washington from The Glen.* 1875 Bierstadt stereoscopic view. From the author's collection.

left the most visible scars in the White Mountains, for there are no visible signs of the pre-historic sea.

Two forms of glacial activity, alpine and continental, have occurred in the White mountains. A "Valley" or "Alpine" glacier was confined to a valley. With the melting of the glaciers, the remaining valley had steep walls and a glacial "cirque," a natural semi-circular design or half bowl shape, as its headwall. Two examples of glacial cirques in the White Mountains are Tuckerman Ravine, on the easterly side of Mt. Washington and King Ravine on the northern side of Mt. Adams. Tuckerman Ravine is visible from Route 16 in Pinkham Notch and King Ravine is visible from Route 2 in Randolph. Valley glaciers were formed from the compacting ice that accumulated there by the drifting snow that was often blown into them from the summits of the mountains. All of the existing glacial cirques in the White Mountains are on the northerly or easterly side of the mountains. This is because the prevailing winds were from west and would have blown the snow into the northern and eastern valleys. The cirques that are visible today, predate the last period of continental glaciation.

The Wisconsin Glaciation was the last continental ice age that climaxed 18,000 -20,000 years ago and left its own very distinct scars in the mountains. During that period, New England was covered with ice a mile thick, and the pre-existing glacial moraines, large piles of rock and sand that had been deposited at the terminus of the Alpine glaciers, were moved away. The

---

*The Glen House and Mount Carter.* Moses F. Sweetser, *Views of the White Mountains.* From the author's collection.

scraping, grinding and gouging actions of the glacier and the rocks being carried by the moving ice mass left easily recognizable scars, large numbers of scour marks or groves, on exposed rock surfaces of the Presidential range. These can be seen on the cliffs on Pine Mountain, to the east of Mt. Madison. Another result of these actions is often a rounded rock surface as can be seen in the rounded dome of Mt. Eisenhower. Another sign of the continental glaciers is the glacial erratic, or large boulders and rocks, moved from where the earth originally created them to new positions and places far from their origins. This glacial erratic may be found on the summits and in the valleys. The flowing water of the melting ice mass also left its marks. The potholes that are found on the Ridge of the Caps Trail on Mt. Jefferson are scars from the running water of the melting glaciers.

There is an apocryphal story of a conversation between a visitor to the mountains and a local farmer. The visitor asked: "How did all these rocks get on Mt. Washington?" "The glacier brought them of course," was the reply. "And what happened to the glacier?" continued the visitor. "Well," the farmer slowly replied, "its gone back for another load." For many years, forest rangers have repeated this story to mountain visitors.

These great and tremendous geologic forces, now dormant, were the instruments that carved and sculpted and thereby transformed the White Mountains into the natural setting that we enjoy today.

---

*Hikers on a path.* Unknown photographer.
New Hampshire Historical Society Collection.

## GIANT'S GRAVE

The Giant's Grave was a large mound of dirt in the area known as Fabyan. The mound was removed when the Fabyan Hotel was constructed. There is a legend that an Indian stood on this mound with a flaming torch lit by a bolt of lightening and proclaimed that: "No pale face shall take deep root here; this the Great Spirit whispered in my ear." The inn once belonging to Ethan Alan Crawford and built here burned, as have all other inns constructed on this site.

## GIBBS BROOK and Gibbs Falls

Gibbs Brook, which comes off of Mt. Clinton (Pierce), on the eastern side of Route 302 in Crawford Notch, is named after Joseph Gibbs who purchased the Crawford House from Thomas Crawford. As a resident of the area, Gibbs acquired an intimate knowledge of the mountain weather that was invaluable to his guests. A guidebook of the time noted that: "But whenever Mr. Gibbs can be induced to give his opinion (about the unpredictable mountain weather), it may be relied upon as correct." Gibbs once owned the Lafayette House near Franconia.

One 19th century guide book described Gibbs Falls as a "junior Yosemite." Gibbs Falls was a popular afternoon walk for the 19th century guests at the Crawford House. On these afternoon walks, men would wear a coat and tie and frequently a fashionable hat. At the same time, the ladies would wear large hooped skirts—by modern standards a most cumbersome form of hiking clothes.

*The Glen Ellis Fall.* Moses F. Sweetser, *Views of the White Mountains.* From the author's collection.

## GLEN

A "Glen" is most often described as a small secluded valley. In the history of the White Mountains, "The Glen" referred to the site of the Glen House, north of Pinkham Notch.

Today "Glen" also refers to the area in Bartlett where Routes 302 and 16 intersect and the Saco River and the Ellis River merge.

## GLEN BOULDER

This is an immense boulder that appears to be rolling down a ridge southeast of Mt. Washington and above Pinkham Notch. In fact, the boulder is sitting securely in its location. Glen Boulder, carried to its present location during the last glacial period, today rests above treeline and is a very visible landmark from Route 16. A steep trail leads up to Glen Boulder from a parking area south of the Glen Ellis Falls. It takes about two hours to walk up to the boulder.

## GLEN ELLIS FALLS

The Ellis River is formed by the convergence of several rivers coming out of Tuckerman Ravine, Huntington Ravine and off of Wildcat Mountain. The origin of the name of the Ellis River is not known. The Sweetser guide notes that Ellis may have been originally spelled "Elise" or "Elis."

Glen Ellis Falls, a waterfall of approximately 70 feet in height, is approximately one mile south of the Pinkham Notch AMC Camp. The Falls are easily accessible by foot from a public parking area (photo page 83).

Formerly known as "Pitcher Falls," because of the way in which the water falls in a narrow and even fashion, resembling water falling from a pitcher, the falls were renamed for unknown reasons in 1852 by a Mr. Henry Shepley, a businessman from Portland, Maine. The 1863 Eastman guide, for unstated reasons, praised the name change and called it "more appropriate." Sweetser's 1891 guide regretted that Shepley had renamed these falls and referred to the new name as "less significant."

Such were the disagreements between the authors of the 19th century guide books .

## GOOSE EYE, MT.
Elevation 3,860

Mt. Goose Eye is located in the Mahoosuc Range east of the city of Berlin. This unusual name is reportedly a derivation of "Goose High," meaning that the geese flew at this height when they passed the mountain in the course of their seasonal migrations.

## GORDON RIDGE and Gordon Falls

James Gordon was a mountain guide who lived in Gorham. The Rev. Starr King frequently employed Gordon as his guide and recommended him in his book *The White Hills* where he wrote that Gordon could be found by asking for a guide at the Alpine House in Gorham. Gordon was described as, "as much at home in the woods as a bear, and who gets along without a compass in their thickets, by having the instinct of a bee."

Gordon is credited with cutting the first trail to the summit of Mt. Madison. Gordon Ridge is one of the ridges on the northern side of that mountain. Gordon Falls is on the Snyder Brook that lies in the valley between Gordon Ridge and Durand Ridge.

## GORHAM, TOWN OF

The town of Gorham is located at the northern base of the White Mountains where the Androscoggin and Peabody rivers merge. Gorham was originally settled as "Shelburne Addition" in 1771 but was incorporated as a town in 1836. The name was suggested by Sylvester Davis, an early settler who was from Gorham, Maine, and was descended from the family that had founded that town.

Prior to the arrival of the railroads, Gorham was little more than a poor farming community with rocky farms and some small logging operations. The Atlantic and St. Lawrence Railroad came to Gorham in 1851. With the arrival of the railroad, the rapidly growing tourist trade found that train connections in Gorham were preferable to the longer stagecoach rides. Tourists from the seacoast and Boston rapidly came through Gorham on their way to the Glen House or other summer hotels. Of Gorham, it was said that the passengers were set "down at the very base of the White Mountains."

The growth of Gorham as a repair center for the Grand Trunk Railway and later the Canadian National continued to contribute to the growth of the town as a railway center. However, like other towns whose economy was centered on the railroad, Gorham's economy declined when the automobile replaced the train as the preferred means of transportation in the twentieth century. Where once the logging industry provided lumber for Gorham's Libby and Peabody lumber companies, today's logging industry feeds the pulp mills in Gorham and Berlin.

*The Great Gulf, Mt. Washington.* Photo by Eugene S. Jones. New Hampshire Historical Society Collection.

## GRAY KNOB CABIN

The Gray Knob Cabin is located just below treeline on the western side of Mt. Adams. Prior to the construction of the cabin Charles Torrey had discovered a spring at this site. The cabin was built in 1906 by E. J. Hincks, a friend of Torrey's, as a private cabin on land that Hincks leased from a lumber company. When the U. S. Forest Service acquired the land, Hincks was given a 25 year lease on the condition that the cabin be open to the public. The Forest Service later gave the cabin to the town of Randolph. The Randolph Mountain Club is today responsible for its maintenance. In 1989 the original cabin was demolished and a new one was built. The Gray Knob cabin is the only shelter on the Presidential range that is staffed year round by a caretaker.

## GREAT GULF, THE

The Great Gulf is located on the northern side of Mt. Washington and is clearly visible from Route 16 near the Glen House site at the base of the Auto Road. Formed during the glacial period, it is possible to stand near the edge of the Gulf and look down into it from the Gulfside Trail as the hiker passes from Mt. Washington to Mt. Clay and over to Mt. Jefferson and Mt. Adams.

Professor Charles Hitchcock described the Great Gulf as being a "great gorge cut out of an ancient plateau, which extended from Boott's Spur to Mt. Madison. The excavation has been formed by the powerful erosive agency of water, acting through a vast space of time."

It is reported that this area was named by Ethan Allen

Crawford one day when he lost his way while guiding some visitors through some bad weather. After wandering for a period, the group found itself at the edge of a "great gulf."

For unknown reasons, early descriptions of the gulf use the name "Gulf of Mexico." That name is not found in modern guides and maps. In 1882 Samuel Drake described the Great Gulf as "like the crater of some mighty volcano on the eve on an eruption vomiting forth volumes of thickening cloud and mist." Professor Huntington called the Great Gulf, the "most monotonous and uninteresting place in the mountains."

Today the Great Gulf is a restricted use area protected under the Wilderness Area Act of 1964.

## GREENLEAF HUT

The Greenleaf Hut, at an elevation of about 4,200 feet on Mt. Lafayette, is a part of the AMC's White Mountain hut system. This hut was built in 1929 with a bequest from Colonel C. H. Greenleaf who began his hotel career as a bellboy at the Profile House, the large summer hotel in Franconia Notch, and later became the proprietor of both that hotel and the Vendome Hotel on Commonwealth Avenue in Boston.

The views from this modest cabin overlook the mountain and notch where the donor lived and worked in a hotel that was one of the most splendid in New Hampshire.

## GULFSIDE TRAIL

This trail, marked by J. Rayner Edmands with cairns (small piles of stones), passes around the Great Gulf from Mt. Washington to the Madison Spring Hut.

## GUYOT, MT. Elevation 4,589

**GUYOT, MT.** Elevation 4,589

Located west of Zealand Notch is Mt. Guyot named after Arnold Henri Guyot, a Swiss scientist who came to the United States in 1848 and became a Professor of Geography at Princeton University in 1854. In 1860 he published a map of the White Mountains. During the summers Guyot widely explored the Appalachian Mountain Range from New England to Georgia. It was his work that proved that Mt. Washington was not the highest peak east of the Mississippi. In addition to this mountain in New Hampshire, there are peaks named after Guyot in New York, Utah, Colorado and California. In addition, a crater on the moon bears his name.

### HALES LOCATION

Hales Location is located west of the town of Conway and is today part of the White Mountain National Forest. In 1771 this area was granted to Major Samuel Hale of the New Hampshire Provincial Army. Hale, a 1740 graduate of Harvard, settled in the City of Portsmouth and died there in 1807. For a period after his death, his heirs continued to live in the Conway area to take care of the grant.

### HALE, MT. Elevation 4,077

Charles Hitchcock, the New Hampshire State Geologist, named this mountain after his friend and fellow explorer the Reverend Edward Everett Hale of Boston. Hale, a Congregational Minister and chaplain to the United States Senate, was also a prominent 19th century author, one of whose works was *The Man Without a Country*. Hale was an early member of the Society for the Protection of New Hampshire Forests.

The Hale Brook Trail ascends this mountain from the Zealand Trail.

## HANCOCK, MT.         Elevation 4,403

Mt. Hancock, named after John Hancock, President of the Continental Congress, is located west of Mt. Carrigain and north of the Kancamagus Highway.

## HARTS LOCATION

Route 302 passes through Harts Location between Crawford Notch and the town of Bartlett. This area was granted to and named after Colonel John Hart of Portsmouth as a reward for his military service during the French and Indian War. This area was the home to Abel Crawford, the "Patriarch of the Mountains," and also to Dr. Samuel Bemis, the "Lord of the Valley." Abel Crawford is buried here.

## HAYES, MT.         Elevation 2,566

Mt. Hayes is located on the eastern side of the Androscoggin River, north of Gorham. There was once a bridle path to the summit of the mountain. Starr King writes that this mountain takes it name from Mrs. Margaret Hayes, the proprietor of the White Mountain Station House in Gorham which later became the Alpine House. King writes, "It is now her mountain." King also described Mt. Hayes as "the chair set by the Creator at the proper distance and angle to appreciate and enjoy his (Mt. Washington's) kingly prominence."

## HIGHT, MT.         Elevation 4,690

The exact source of the name for this mountain, located

between Carter Dome and South Carter in the Carter Range, is not certain. In 1797 there was a farmer named James Hight in the town of Jefferson.

Sweetser's guide includes what is described as a legend about two hunters named Carter and Hight who were once trapping together in the region. When they became separated, they climbed to the peaks above them. Reportedly, Carter climbed to the summit of what is now Carter Dome and Hight climbed to the peak of what is now Wildcat Mountain. For a period of time that mountain was known as Mt. Hight. When the name was changed to "Wild-Cat Mountain" by Professor Arnold Guyot of Princeton, some people wanted to preserve the Hight name. Thus, Sweetser concludes the peak to the north of Carter Dome was renamed Mt. Hight.

## HINCKS TRAIL

The Hincks Trail, cleared by E. J. Hincks, goes from the Spur Trail to the Gray Knob Cabin on Nowell Ridge. (See Gray Knob Cabin.)

## HITCHCOCK FALLS and Mt. Hitchcock          Elevation 3,648

The Hitchcock Falls are located on Bumpus Brook on the northeast side of Mt. Madison. These falls are along the Howker Ridge Trail. Mt. Hitchcock is located north of the Kancamagus Highway and west of Mt. Hancock. There are no trails on Mt. Hitchcock.

---

*Advertisement for the Profile House, Franconia Notch. Chisholm's White Mountain Guide, 1880. From the author's collection.*

# ❃PROFILE HOUSE❃

## Franconia Notch, White Mountains, N.H.

### (The largest Hotel in New England.)

## TAFT & GREENLEAF, Proprietors.

#### C. H. GREENLEAF, of The Vendome, Boston.

## Open from June 20th to October 1st.

##### POST-OFFICE ADDRESS: PROFILE HOUSE, N.H

---

**How to Reach the Profile House.**—ALL Rail, and through in one day from Boston, Newport, New York, Saratoga, Lake George, Montreal, Quebec, Portland, etc., via Profile and Franconia Notch R.R. from Bethlehem Junction: or by DAILY STAGES, via Flume House to Pemigewasset Valley R.R.,—10 miles,—connecting with trains to and from Boston, New York, and all points.

## EXCURSIONS.

### OBSERVATION WAGONS THROUGH THE NOTCH TWICE DAILY,
##### FOR
# OLD MAN OF THE MOUNTAIN,
## FLUME, POOL, BASIN,
##### AND ALL POINTS OF INTEREST.

Guests, by taking the morning train on the Profile and Franconia Notch Railroad, can visit the Summit of MT. WASHINGTON, or go through the WHITE MOUNTAIN NOTCH to NORTH CONWAY, or visit JEFFERSON or BETHLEHEM, and returning, reach Profile House by rail same day.

**Good Bridle and Foot-Paths** to the summit of Lafayette, Cannon and Bald Mountains: also, pleasant walks to the Cascade and Echo and Profile Lakes. Upon Echo Lake a small steamer, and upon both Lakes safe row-boats can be had.

**The Stables are supplied with the best of Livery and Saddle Horses.**

Charles H. Hitchcock was the first state geologist in New Hampshire and for 40 years was a Professor at Dartmouth College.

It has also been suggested that the Hitchcock Falls were named in honor of Colonel John R. Hitchcock, the manager of both the Alpine House in Gorham and the Tip Top House on Mt. Washington and one of the founders of the Mt. Washington Carriage (Auto) Road. In 1869 Colonel Hitchcock refused Professor Hitchcock's request for use of the summit buildings on Mt. Washington for winter research. The following year Professor Hitchcock received permission from the Cog Railway to use their buildings. The two Hitchcocks were unrelated.

## HOTELS IN THE WHITE MOUNTAINS

Today's White Mountain visitor stays in very modest and simple hotels and motels when compared with the grandeur of the hotels that stood here in the 19th century but have today passed into obscurity. These large hotels were built to serve the demands of the thousands of tourists who visited the White Mountains for extended periods of time, very often the entire summer, during the last century.

The very earliest "hotel accommodations" were the private farms and taverns that were spread throughout the area. In these inns the kitchen, the bar, the living room, and the dining room were most often all the same room. The "guests" most often spent the night either in a drafty attic or on the floor in front of the fire.

*The Profile House*. Moses F. Sweetser, *Views of the White Mountains*. From the author's collection.

# HOTELS

Lucy Crawford described her home, an early inn, as follows:

> As our house was so small we could not accommodate but a few at a time, although we could give them clean beds; but they were obliged to stow closely at night, and near the roof, as we had but two small sleeping rooms down stairs, and these were generally occupied by ladies; the gentlemen were under the necessity of going up stairs, and there lay so near each other, that their beds nearly touched; but as we did all we could for them, they seemed satisfied with it.

Another early innkeeper was Samuel W. Thompson, a mail carrier of North Conway. In the 1830's he started to run his house as an inn for the teamsters who were traveling through North Conway with their commerce. Thompson's son was to describe living in this inn as follows: "There was hardly a night but our little house was not taxed to its utmost capacity." At a later date, after the railroad allowed the freight to pass through without stopping, Thompson's clientele would change and he provided summer accommodations for the artists who came to the mountains.

As more and more people came to the mountains, as a result of changes in transportation and the introduction of passenger train service to the area, the need for larger and better hotels was quickly recognized. Some of the railroads built hotels to accommodate the passengers that they were taking to the mountains.

Only the Mt. Washington Hotel at Bretton Woods survives as the last of these great hotels. This hotel, built by Joseph

---

*Advertisement for the Maplewood Hotel, Bethlehem, New Hampshire. Chisholm's White Mountain Guide, 1880. From the author's collection.*

WHITE MOUNTAINS.

"THE MAPLEWOOD,"

MAPLEWOOD, BETHLEHEM, N. H.

Stickney, must seem as grand today with its Spanish Renaissance style and large octagonal towers at each end as it did when it opened in 1902. At that time, guests were charged $5.00 per night or between $21 and $35 per week, and the hotel could accommodate over 550 visitors. The Mount Washington Hotel was the site of the 1944 Bretton Woods Monetary Conference at which the World Bank was established, the gold standard was set at $35 per ounce, and the U. S. dollar was determined to be the basis of international exchange.

To fully appreciate the hotels that stood here in the White Mountains there are other statistics and descriptions that should be considered. In 1902, in the seven towns of Randolph, Jefferson, Carroll, Bethlehem, Conway, Jackson, and Gorham, there were over 75 hotels that could accommodate over 7,400 guests. Sweetser claims that it was possible for over 14,000 guests to be housed in the White Mountains in accommodations ranging from simple farms to grand hotels.

The Profile House in Franconia Notch was built in 1902. At that time, it could accommodate between 500 and 600 guests at a cost of $5.00 per night. The Sweetser Guide describes this hotel as follows: "There are post and telegraph offices, billiard balls and bowling alleys, bathrooms, a barber shop, a salesroom for pictures and knick-knacks, a livery stable, passenger elevator and four tennis courts." The Chisholm guide described the Profile House dining room, which served grapes that were raised in the hotel's greenhouses, as "fit for a conclave of

*Arriving with the Summer Luggage.* Photo by Willis Boyd Allen. Probably taken at the Crawford House. New Hampshire Historical Society Collection.

Cardinals." On one occasion, P. T. Barnum produced a very special "circus" at the Profile House in which Barnum's employees were dressed as animals to entertain the guests.

The town of Bethlehem, with its two mile boardwalk, became famous as a retreat for people suffering from hay fever. The main street of this town was lined with large hotels, all of which are now gone. The Maplewood Hotel in Bethlehem maintained its own 600 acre farm to supply the hotel with milk products and fresh vegetables. At the intersection of Routes 3 and 302 in the town of Carroll, east of Bethlehem, was the Twin Mountain House which could house over 200 guests. This hotel was recommended by the U. S. Hay Fever Association because its altitude was above the "hay fever line." (See Beecher Cascade.) Similarly, the Glen House advertised that visitors there would be free of "Rose Cold and Hay Fever." People who suffered from hay fever quickly recognized the truth of these claims, that the altitudes of the White Mountains were free from hay fever.

By 1902 the town of Jefferson, which Starr King had once described as a town with "great potential" for a hotel, had not one, but seven hotels that could provide for over 750 guests. The largest of these was the Waumbek with room for over 500 guests who, if they came by train, would be brought directly to the hotel grounds in the railroad parlor cars. The Alpine House in Gorham was directly across from the Railway Station and would often be a stop for visitors before they headed to either the Glen House or other hotels. The Glen House, because of its proximity to Gorham and the trains, was a favorite hotel. The first Glen House was built in 1870 and, after a number of expansions, could accommodate over 500 guests. From its 700 foot long "piazzas" the guests could look out towards the

Presidential Range. The Glen House maintained a stable of 100 horses for stages and other general purposes. The first Glen House (photo page 79) burned in 1884. A second was built in 1885, but that burned in 1893. A third Glen House was built, but that burned in 1924. This third hotel was replaced by a fourth hotel, but it too was destroyed by fire.

There was one hotel at the top of Mt. Washington, The Summit House. This hotel, built in 1902 by Walter Aiken, the manager of the Cog Railway, could accommodate 150 guests who wanted to see both a sunset and a sunrise from the summit of the mountain. Aiken's building was the first summit structure that provided any services for visitors to the top of Mt. Washington. Fire destroyed this hotel in 1908. Consideration was then given to building a much larger hotel and a larger train to the summit. The plan was abandoned, and a smaller hotel reopened on the summit in 1915. In 1968 that hotel stopped taking overnight guests. It has been torn down.

These large hotels were primarily summer inns, opening in June and closing in October after the fall foliage. A few, including the Ravine House in Randolph, operated by Laban Watson, were open in the winter to accommodate those few individuals who wanted to experience winter hiking.

These grand hotels are today only history. A combination of better roads, fires and changes in personal vacation patterns brought about the demise of these businesses. After some of the fires, hotels were rebuilt, only to burn again at a later date. Perhaps the greatest hotel fire was the August 3, 1923 fire at the Profile House. Within a four-hour period, the hotel and 25 buildings around it were consumed by fire. There were no casualties, and no cause was ever positively identified.

One common characteristic of all of these White Mountain Hotels was the large collection of rocking chairs that were available on each porch or piazza and the resulting rocking chair brigades that occupied them, spreading a constant supply of gossip to and amongst the summer visitors. Gossip would originate at one hotel and then quickly be spread around the mountains. With each repetition of the "news" there was undoubtedly a slight change to the story. Thus, by the time that the "news" had made a complete circumference of the mountains, for example, from the Glen House, to Gorham, to Randolph, and then to Jefferson and then to Twin Mountain and Crawford Notch, and then to Bartlett, to continue to Jackson and finally arrive back at the Glen House, the story would have undergone such a complete metamorphosis that it would not be recognizable by its originator, who if he or she heard it, would have thought it to be new and repeated it to yet another person, thereby sending the "same" story around the mountain again.

## HOWKER RIDGE

Howker Ridge leads from the Dolly Copp Road to the summit of Mt. Madison. The rocky knobs along this ridge, visible from Route 2 in Randolph, have come to be known as "howks." The James Howker family were early farmers in the town of Randolph. Two trails ascend Mt. Madison via the Howker Ridge. The Howker Ridge Trail begins at the Randolph East parking area on the Dolly Copp road while the Pine Link Trail begins at the Dolly Copp Road opposite the road leading up Pine Mountain.

The Howker Ridge Trail was cleared by Charles Torrey,

Professor of Semitic Languages at Yale University, one of the early path builders who summered in Randolph. One day, in order to get a better view while clearing this trail, Torrey climbed a yellow birch. Upon reaching the top of the tree, the branch broke and Torrey fell to the ground, breaking his ankle in two places. A brother, who was working with him, covered Torrey with the spare clothing and went for help. Thunderstorms during the night slowed the rescue efforts of the two groups from Randolph who eventually located Torrey, tied him to a makeshift stretcher, and brought him down the mountain. Torrey limped for the rest of his life as a result of this injury.

## HUNTINGTON RAVINE and
## Mt. Huntington
Elevation 3,670

Located on the eastern side of Mt. Washington, Huntington Ravine has a very steep cliff as its headwall. This cliff, the steepest trail up Mt. Washington, is clearly visible from Route 16 as the road passes through Pinkham Notch.

The ravine is named in honor of J. H. Huntington who was an early participant in winter research on the summit of Mt. Washington. In 1858, Huntington, a graduate of Amherst College, was working with Dartmouth College Professor Charles Hitchcock near Lake Champlain. During the summer Huntington expressed his interest in spending a winter studying the arctic conditions on the summit of Washington.

It was not until 1869 that funds became available to conduct this research, but Huntington could not get the approval needed to use the buildings at the summit of Mt. Washington that belonged to the Carriage Road company. Not wanting to abandon his project, Huntington spent the winter of 1869-1870

on the summit of Mt. Moosilauke with the assistance of Dartmouth College. The publicity from this research made it easier to gain the funds and approval to spend the following winter, 1870-1871, on the summit of Mt. Washington using buildings belonging to the Cog Railway.

Mt. Huntington, located north of the Kancamagus Highway and south of Mt. Hancock, is named in honor of the same person.

## ICE GULCH

The Ice Gulch is a narrow gulch on the side of Mt. Crescent in Randolph. Even in the middle of the summer, ice may be found under the immense boulders that lie here. The walk through the "chambers" of the Ice Gulch is very difficult, over and under the massive boulders.

## IMP, THE

The Imp, a cliff profile on North Carter, is visible from both Route 16 and the Dolly Copp Campground. Sweetser's guide describes The Imp as "a grotesque colossal sphinx." During the mid 1800's it was occasionally referred to as "Dolly's Imp," a reference to Dolly Copp.

## INDIAN HEAD

The Indian Head profile, a rocky ledge, is on Mt. Pemigewasset at the southern end of Franconia Notch on the western side of Route 3.

---

*The Imp.* Samuel A. Drake. From the author's collection.

## INGALLS, MT. Elevation 2,253

Mt. Ingalls is at the southern end of the Mahoosuc Range above the village of Shelburne. Daniel Ingalls and several other members of his family were the first settlers of Shelburne, arriving there between 1770 and 1772.

## INTERVALE

An intervale is specifically defined as the flat low-lying land along a stream. This very general definition applies to many of the streams throughout northern New Hampshire. However, in the White Mountains "Intervale" also refers to an area just north of North Conway from where there is a panoramic view of the Presidential Range. Many artists painted the hills from this area, and today it is preserved as it was a century ago because it is in the flood plain where development is not possible. Because of the economic impact the artists painting this specific location have had on the White Mountain tourist industry, these low lying fields may strangely be considered to be a vital part of the economic history of northern New Hampshire.

## IRON MOUNTAIN Elevation 2,716

As its name suggests, Iron Mountain in Jackson was the location of a rich iron mine. In 1891 Sweetser described the "inexhaustible quantities of iron" that could be found here. Iron is no longer mined at this site.

## ISRAEL RIVER and Israel Ridge

Prior to 1750, two trappers, John and Israel Glines, brothers, visited and hunted in northern New Hampshire and the White Mountains. The Israel River, named after one of the brothers, flows northwesterly through the towns of Jefferson and Lancaster. A later visit to the region by a group led by Captain Peter Powers caused that group to name the river the "Powers River." Despite a description of Israel Glines as a "worthless trapper" by a 19th century writer, the newer but still 18th century name "Powers River" was never accepted.

The Israel Ridge, on the northwest side of Mt. Jefferson, was named by J. Rayner Edmands because it is near the source of the Israel River.

## JACKSON, MT.                                    Elevation 4,052

Mt. Jackson, located above Crawford Notch between Mt. Webster and Mr. Clinton (Pierce), can be climbed from Crawford Notch.

Mt. Jackson is not named in honor of President Jackson but after Charles Thomas Jackson who in 1838 was named the New Hampshire State Geologist and who then did much research in the Presidential Range. William Oakes is credited with having named this mountain.

## JACKSON, TOWN OF

The town of Jackson is located at the southern end of Pinkham Notch. The town was first known as New Madbury after the town of Madbury in southern New Hampshire. One of the first settlers was Captain Joseph Pinkham of Madbury. He and his family moved north in the winter of 1790, with their furniture and other possessions packed on a sled pulled by a pig. When they arrived at their log cabin, the family found it nearly covered with snow.

When the town was incorporated in 1800, the name was

changed to Adams in honor of the second President, John Adams. In 1829 the name was changed again, to Jackson. This last change was reportedly made because all but one of the town's inhabitants had voted for Andrew Jackson over John Quincy Adams in the election of 1828.

### JEFFERSON, MT. Elevation 5,715

Located between Mt. Clay and Mt. Adams is Mt. Jefferson, named in honor of the third President, Thomas Jefferson. (See Presidential Range.)

### JEFFERSON, TOWN OF

The town of Jefferson, formerly named Dartmouth, was granted to Colonel John Goffe in 1765. Goffe never fulfilled the requirements of his grant and over time, Colonel Joseph Whipple of Portsmouth obtained ownership of almost the entire town. In 1796, the town was incorporated as Jefferson, named after Thomas Jefferson before he became President.

The town was not settled until Colonel Whipple came to this area through Crawford Notch. Different sources give the date of Whipple's arrival as either 1772 or 1773. After making his fortune in Portsmouth, New Hampshire, in the sailing industry Whipple acquired the rights to most of the town of Jefferson, which he proceeded to manage as a small fiefdom. It has been written that when he moved to Jefferson, he took several slaves with him. During the American Revolution the Whipple home was attacked by a group of Indians. Whipple asked to be excused so that he could change his clothes before leaving the farm, but when he was alone in a back room Whipple escaped through a window.

The Indians proceeded to plunder the house. Whipple, a local businessman, made an annual trip to Portland, Maine, to trade for himself and others living in Jefferson. It is reported that on at least one trip he returned with a bag of half-pennies so that he could be certain that he made the exact change for everyone. Whipple Brook, in the northern section of Jefferson is named in his honor.

Another early settler in Jefferson was Deborah Vickers who would become known as "Granny Stalbird" (sometimes Stabbard or Starbird). In 1776, Granny Stalbird was the first white woman to climb through what would become known as Crawford Notch on her way to work on the Whipple farm. In her later years, Granny Stalbird became a North Country doctoress who took care of the settlers in the area. She once examined Ethan Allen Crawford's wound after he had injured himself with an ax. Upon removing the bandages, the injury opened and began to bleed. As Granny had been trained by the Indians in the use of the local herbs and roots, she went into the field and collected young clover leaves. She then pounded them into a mortar and placed them on Crawford's wound. Crawford claimed that this treatment so suddenly stopped the bleeding that he fainted. Before it was destroyed by the builders of the Grand Trunk Railway, there was a ledge in Shelburne named after Granny Stalbird. On one visit to a patient in Shelburne, she and her horse were forced to take shelter under this ledge because of a bad storm. Stalbird Brook, on the western side of Jefferson, remembers this early White Mountain pioneer.

Starr King wrote of Jefferson that, "if a good hotel should be erected there, the village would soon become one of the most popular resorts among the mountains." Later, inns would be built in Jefferson, and it would become a popular summer community. (See Hotels In The White Mountains.)

## JEFFERSON NOTCH ROAD

This road, first opened in 1902, passes between the Cog Railway Base Station and the town of Jefferson. In the course of passing through the "notch" between Mts. Bowman, Jefferson, and Clay to the east and Mts. Mitten, Dartmouth, and Deception to the west, the road reaches an elevation of 3,011 feet.

## JEWELL TRAIL

The Jewell Trail ascends Mt. Washington from the Base Station of the Cog Railway. This trail was named for Sergeant W. S. Jewell of Lisbon, New Hampshire, who was in charge of the Mt. Washington Observatory during the years 1878-1880.

## JOHN'S RIVER

John's River runs through the town of Whitefield and Dalton, to the Connecticut River. There are several stories about the origin of the name.

The most commonly accepted origin is that it is named after John Glines, a local hunter. There were two brothers, John and Israel Glines. This river honors John while the Israel River and the Israel Ridge remember his brother.

Another story is that John's River was formerly known as the John Stark River after Ensign John Stark, later in the Revolutionary War to become General John Stark, the most prominent military man in New Hampshire. Stark was twice captured by the Indians during his hunting trips. When he was first captured at the age of 21, Stark was told by his captors to hoe the corn. Stark gained the respect of the Indians by throwing the hoe onto the ground and declaring that that was the work for the squaws. General Stark gained great fame with his defeat of the British forces at the Battle of Bennington, a Revolutionary War battle fought by New Hampshire soldiers in the state of New York, but named after a Vermont town that had been named after Benning Wentworth, the Royal Governor of New Hampshire. It is General Stark who is credited with having included the phrase "Live Free or Die" in a letter to a friend. This has become the New Hampshire state motto. While there may be doubt as to whether this river was named after Ensign John Stark, the town of Stark, north of Berlin, was named after General Stark.

In either event, the last name of whomever this river was intended to honor has been abandoned in favor of only the first name.

## KANCAMAGUS HIGHWAY and
### Kancamagus, Mt.                    Elevation 3,728

The Kancamagus Highway is a 34½ mile highway between North Woodstock and Conway. The highway, parts of which date to 1837, has today been designated a National Scenic Byway. Along the roadside there are a number of picnic areas, hiking trails, and campgrounds.

Mt. Kancamagus, named by Professor Huntington, is south of Mt. Huntington and the Kancamagus Highway.

Chief Kancamagus, "The Fearless One," led the 1686 Indian raid on Dover. After that, he retreated to Canada and was not heard from again. He was the grandson of Chief Passaconaway.

## KEARSARGE, MT.                              Elevation 3,268

From the summit of pyramid shaped Mt. Kearsarge, east of North Conway, there are views of the Presidential Range and on very clear days, the Atlantic Ocean. Mt. Kearsarge, formerly spelled Kiarsarge, was known by the Indians as Pequawket.

The exact derivation of "Kearsarge" is uncertain. It may be from the Abenaki word "Kesarzet" meaning "Pointed Mountain" or "High Place" or "Land that is Harsh and Difficult." Others have suggested that it is from the Algonquin word "Kesough" meaning, "Born of the Hill that First Shakes Hands with the Morning Light," a reference to the fact that sunlight will reach the peak of the mountain before it reaches the valley below. Others have suggested that there was a local hunter, Hezekiah Sargent in this area in the mid-1700's. The name "Kearsarge" name may be a contraction of his name: "Kiah Sarges Mountain."

The Reverend Starr King described Kearsarge as the "queenly mountain" and believed that it should have been named after Martha Washington. During the mid 1800's there was a bridle path to the summit of the mountain. A hotel was built on the summit in 1845, but it was blown down in 1883. A smaller building built the following year is no longer there.

## KILKENNY

The Kilkenny is a large wild region north of Randolph and Jefferson. The region was never actively settled and is today almost as wild as it was when white settlers first came to

*Lakes of the Clouds.* Postcard from the New Hampshire Historical Society Collection.

northern New Hampshire. Perhaps the greatest human activity in this region took place between 1887 and 1897 when the Lancaster & Kilkenny Railway Company operated a logging train here. Today, one can only wonder if the name was transferred here from Kilkenny County in Ireland by one of the very few settlers to have ever lived here.

### KING RAVINE and
### Starr King Mountain                         Elevation 3,913

Thomas Starr King was a Unitarian clergyman who made frequent visits to the White Mountains, during which he wrote prolifically. At first these writings were letters, but he was to later turn them into the famous book *The White Hills: Their Legends, Landscape and Poetry*. This book, first published in 1871 when King was 36, is credited with having brought many visitors to the White Mountains to see the area that he so vividly described. King's book is a combination guidebook, historical sketch, poetry and religious passages about the majesty of the mountains. (King's book was republished in 1991 by Heritage Books.) One biographer has written that King, "felt the thrill of a romanticist, the quiet ecstasy of the aesthete and the deep rapture of a truly religious man."

In later years, King was to explore the mountains of California. Starr King Mountain in Jefferson, New Hampshire, and King Ravine on the northern side of Mt. Adams are the two areas that remember this writer and explorer in the White Mountains. In California there is a Mount Starr King in the Yosemite Valley.

When describing "the ravine of Mt. Adams," King said that it was "the grandest of all of the gorges that have been cloven out of the White Hills." Starr King explored "the ravine of Mount

Adams," later to become King Ravine, with his friend and guide James Gordon. Of that expedition, King wrote that this ravine was "grander than Tuckerman's." He described its "deep divinity —the sweep of its keen-edged walls from the very shoulders of the mountain to its feet by the Randolph road." Chisholm's guidebook was to describe this ravine as "paved with the ruins of dismantled ridges and sheltering masses of profound shadow."

## KINSMAN NOTCH and Mt. Kinsman        Elevation 4,363

Asa Kinsman, after whom this notch and mountain south of Franconia are named, came to this area in the early 1780's and made his farm in the town of Easton, east of Franconia.

## LAFAYETTE, MT.                        Elevation 5,242

Mt Lafayette is a part of the Franconia Ridge and was named for the French General, the Marquis de Lafayette in about 1825 at the time of his visit to America. Prior to that, it had been known as Great Haystack. At one time there was a bridle path to the summit.

## LAKES OF THE CLOUDS

The Lakes of the Clouds are small lakes on the western side of Mt. Washington near treeline at the edge of the Ammonoosuc Ravine. These two lakes were carved by the last continental ice sheet and today form the uppermost headwaters of the Ammonoosuc River.

In 1915 a stone hut shelter was built here to provide protection for hikers. The original hut has been expanded by the AMC to become the Lakes of the Clouds Hut which can now accommodate 90 guests.

In some early accounts of these lakes they are referred to as "Washington's Punch Bowl." For several years, the Lakes of the Clouds were known as Blue Pond. This name was given to the lakes after a group led by Ethan Allen Crawford stopped here for a drink. It was said that some of the hikers turned "blue" from the cold water.

**LIBERTY TRAIL.** See Brook Trail.

**LINCOLN, MT.**                                     Elevation 5,108

Mt. Lincoln, in the Franconia Range between Little Haystack and Mt. Lafayette was named after President Lincoln.

**LINCOLN, TOWN OF**

The town of Lincoln, to the south of the Franconia Range, was named in 1764 for the Earl of Lincoln, a cousin of Governor Wentworth.

**LINK TRAIL**

This trail was cleared by J. Rayner Edmands in 1893. It serves as a "link" between the Ravine House and other paths on Nowell Ridge, Israel Ridge and the Castellated Ridge.

**LION HEAD**

This is one of several rock ledges that appears to resemble a figure or animal in the White Mountains. From the Glen House site at the base of the Auto Road, these ledges on a spur between Tuckerman Ravine and Huntington Ravine have the appearance of a lion. At one time they were referred to as "St. Anthony's Nose."

## LITTLE HAYSTACK                    Elevation 4,513

Little Haystack Mountain is located between Mt. Liberty and Mt. Lincoln on the Franconia Ridge. The peaks on this ridge, now bearing the names of Liberty, Lincoln, Lafayette, and Garfield, were all originally called "Haystacks" because they resembled piles of hay when seen from the town of Lincoln, New Hampshire to the south. Only this mountain retains its original name.

## LIVERMORE, TOWN OF

The town of Livermore was named after the Livermore family of Holderness. Samuel Livermore went to Holderness in 1765 and at one time owned half of that town. Livermore was the Attorney General in New Hampshire before the Revolution, a delegate to the Continental Congress, Chief Justice of the New Hampshire Supreme Court, and later a U.S. Senator from New Hampshire. The Livermore Falls are located on the Pemigewasset River about two miles above Plymouth. Mt. Livermore, in the Squam Range, was named for Mary Jane Livermore, the granddaughter of Samuel Livermore.

Livermore, east of Lincoln, did not become an official town until 1876 when it was created by the New Hampshire legislature. It was a company town that served the lumber industry that was cutting this area of New Hampshire's virgin forest. At its height the town had a population of between 150 and 200 in addition to the loggers. The last inhabitant left Livermore in 1949 and the state legislature voted the town out of existence in 1951, 75 years after it had been established. Today, Livermore is entirely located within the White Mountain National Forest, and it is very difficult to find any evidence that it ever existed. A driver along the Kancamagus Highway will pass through this "town" between Conway and Lincoln.

### LOWELL, MT.                                    Elevation 3,743

Mt. Lowell, south of Mt. Anderson near Carrigain Notch is named for Abner Lowell, an explorer of the White Mountains, from Portland, Maine. Sweetser writes that this was formerly known as Brickhouse Mountain.

### LOWES PATH

Lowes Path, the oldest footpath leading up the Presidential Range from the town of Randolph, ascends Nowell Ridge on Mt. Adams from near Lowe's Store on Route 2. When this path was built, between 1875 and 1876 by Charles E. Lowe and Dr. William Nowell, it was a toll path.

Charles Lowe, a descendent of Levi Lowe, one of the earliest settlers in Randolph, was reportedly one of the best guides in the northern peaks. In later years Lowe owned and managed the Mt. Crescent House, a 75 guest hotel on Randolph Hill.

### MADISON, MT.                                    Elevation 5,363

This mountain, to the east of Mt. Adams, is named in honor of James Madison, the fourth President of the United States. (See Presidential Range.)

---

*Mountain-Railway Station in Staging Times.* Marshfield.
Samuel A. Drake. From the author's collection.

## MADISON SPRING HUT

Located in the col between Mt. Madison and Mt. Adams, the Madison Spring Hut is the oldest hut maintained by the AMC in the White Mountains. In 1888, on land given to the AMC by a lumber company, a small rectangular cabin was constructed here with stone walls two feet thick and very simple accommodations for up to twenty-four persons. The original hut had been proposed and actively supported by a group of AMC members that visited Randolph and who viewed this new shelter as an exciting and adventurous place to go for the night. Laban Watson, the proprietor of the Ravine House in Randolph, contributed to the planning and building. In 1906, a second room was added to the original hut and the AMC hired a caretaker to maintain the hut and prepare meals for overnight guests. Five years later a second building was constructed to serve as a cook house. The hut was again enlarged in both 1922 and 1929. An accidental fire in October 1940 destroyed the hut. By August 1941 a new hut had been built under the direction of Joe Dodge.

## MARSHFIELD

Marshfield, also known as the Base Station, is where the Cog Railway is located. This "community" was cut from the forest wilderness by the workmen who built the railway up Mt. Washington.

The name "Marshfield" is the coupling of two names thereby honoring two pioneers on Mt. Washington. "Marsh" honors Sylvester Marsh who conceived of the Cog Railway. Darby Field, who in 1642 became the first person to climb Mt. Washington, is the second person remembered in this name.

## MITTEN, MT.
Elevation 3,050

There are no trails to the summit of this mountain which lies north of Mt. Dartmouth in the Dartmouth Range, to the west of the Jefferson Notch Road in the town of Jefferson.

The Sweetser guide states that this mountain was named for a mitten that an early "visitor" lost on the mountain. William Oakes wrote that the mitten was lost by one of the early "prospectors" of the road through Crawford Notch. Lucy Crawford has written that it was Timothy Nash who lost his mitten here when he climbed a tree to get a better view of the surrounding area. It can only be speculated that Nash accepted that his lost mitten was small in comparison to the grant of land, Nash and Sawyer Location, that he received as a reward for finding Crawford Notch.

## MIZPAH SPRING HUT

This AMC hut, south of Mt. Clinton and built in 1965, houses 65 overnight guests. It has been written that "Mizpah" is an Indian name meaning "Pillar in the Wilderness." The Bible is the more likely source for this name. Mizpah is a Hebrew word meaning "watchtower" and there are several places in Palestine that bear this name.

This hut can be reached quickly by trails leading up from Crawford Notch.

## MOAT MT.
Elevation 3,201

Moat Mountain is located north of the Kancamagus Highway and west of North Conway above Echo Lake. The origins of this name are obscure and may very simply be derived from the beaver dams or "moats" that were once at the bottom of the

mountain. The Abenaki name for this mountain was "Atieompskeaooedi," "A sleeping or lodging place of animals among standing or upright rocks."

Geologically these are some of the newer mountains in the White Mountains. They were formed by the volcanic activity about 175 million years ago which resulted in much of central New Hampshire being covered by volcanic rock. Most of that rock has been eroded away. The rocks that form Moat Mountain, and are found in a few other locations, have come to be called "Moat Volcanic Rocks" after this mountain.

## MONROE, MT.                                    Elevation 5,385

Mt. Monroe the first peak south-west of Mount Washington, was named in honor of President James Monroe, the fifth President of the United States. (See Presidential Range.)

## MONTALBAN RIDGE

This ridge extends southerly from the summit of Mt. Washington. The name is the very simple anglicization of the Latin "Mons," Mountain and "Albus," White or White Mountain. Along the ridge are the summits of several mountains: Isolation, Davis, Stairs, Resolution, and Crawford.

## MONTICELLO LAWN

The southern grassy slope of the summit of Mt. Jefferson is known as the Monticello Lawn, an allusion to Thomas Jefferson's Virginia home. Hikers passing along the Gulfside Trail will walk through this area. At one time, a rusty hand lawnmower

---

*Franconia Iron Works.* Samuel A. Drake.
From the author's collection.

stood in the middle of the "lawn," a humorous contribution to the alpine area by an unknown person.

## MORIAH, MT.

Elevation 4,047

Located south east of Gorham, Sweetser writes that Mt. Moriah was named by an early settler after the hill of the same name in Jerusalem.

## NANCY, MT., Nancy Pond, Nancy Brook, and Nancy Cascade

Elevation 3,906

These four locations are located approximately six miles south of Crawford Notch and four miles above Bartlett. The story behind these names is one of heroism, devotion, betrayal and death.

Nancy Barton was a girl who was employed at the farm of Colonel Joseph Whipple in Jefferson. After becoming engaged to another of the workers on the farm, she gave her entire dowry to him. He then left the farm and abandoned her. Even though this was in the middle of the winter, Nancy followed him to Crawford Notch but found the campfire cold. Nancy continued her search through Crawford Notch but became exhausted and fell beside the brook. Another group of men from Jefferson went to search for Nancy and found her frozen body in the snow. Upon hearing of Nancy's death, her lover reportedly went insane and died a few years later. Tradition says that his ghost is still in the valley.

Mt. Nancy has also been known as Mt. Amorisgelu, Latin for

*Nancy.* Samuel A. Drake. From the author's collection.

"the frost of love." When this name has been infrequently used, the accent is on the third syllable to suggest an Indian name.

## NELSON CRAG and Nelson Crag Trail

The Nelson Crag Trail goes from the Auto Road up and over Nelson Crag and to the Alpine Gardens above Huntington Ravine. S. A. Nelson, of Georgetown, Massachusetts, was one of the men who spent the winter of 1870-1871 doing scientific research on the summit of Mt. Washington. Another scientist to participate in that arctic research was J. H. Huntington.

## NOTCHLAND

When Samuel Bemis built his large house in Harts Location south of Crawford Notch, he gave it this name. For many years, the house was operated as an inn called the Inn Unique. Today the inn is again known by the name that Bemis gave to his home and to this area.

## NOWELL RIDGE

Nowell Ridge is located on the north westerly side of Mt. Adams. Many trails cross this ridge ascending the mountain.

This ridge is named for Dr. William Grey Nowell, a summer resident of Randolph and frequent contributor of articles on the White Mountains to the AMC publication *Appalachia*. Nowell was an active path builder, and in 1890 he built a shelter at the present site of the Log Cabin, and RMC shelter.

In Volume I, Number 1 of *Appalachia*, Nowell presented a long list of "Improvements" that the AMC planned for the White Mountains—both the building of new paths and the restoration of old ones.

## OAKES GULF

Oakes Gulf is the ravine to the southeast of Mt. Monroe.

This area was named by Edward Tuckerman in honor of William Oakes, who first visited the White Mountains in 1825. Oakes, a botanist, spent his many visits searching for botanical specimens. However, he is best remembered for his book *Scenery of the White Mountains*, published in 1848, which was illustrated with large lithographic plates. Oakes was only 49 when he published this book. He died five days after it was accepted for publication in an unexplained drowning off of a Boston ferry boat. Oakes also named Mt. Clay and Mt. Jackson.

## OLD MAST ROAD

The Old Mast Road is a trail leading up Mt. Passaconaway from Route 113A. This trail was reportedly used to transport masts for the Royal Navy before the American Revolution.

When the original Royal Grants were made for the towns of northern New Hampshire, the tall white pines suitable for ship masts were reserved for the Royal Navy. These trees were defined as being 120 feet in height, 40 inches in diameter and "unblemished throughout the entire length." After being hauled to the sea by up to 88 oxen, these masts were transported back to England on special "mast ships."

## ORE HILL                                    Elevation 1,900

Between the towns of Franconia and Sugar Hill, to the west of N. H. Route 116, is a small mountain called Ore Hill. A large and rich vein of iron ore was discovered here after the American Revolution, and it was actively mined until the middle of 19th century. After being blasted from the granite, the ore was transported to the foundries that were built in the village of Franconia where pig and bar iron was produced and then used for farm tools, the Franconia stove, and other cast iron products (photo page 124). At a later date, small amounts of gold were found in the quartz in the neighboring town of Lisbon.

## OSCAR, MT.      Elevation 2,748

This mountain, located in the Rosebrook Range, is named in honor of Oscar Barron, the long time manager of the Fabyan House. At different times, members of the Barron family managed or owned Fabyan House, the Crawford House, the Twin Mountain House, the Mt. Pleasant House, and the Summit House. Oscar Barron's brother, Asa T. Barron, was the first member of the family to go to the White Mountains. The family owned a poultry farm in Quechee, Vermont, and a hotel in White River Junction, Vermont. They quickly recognized that the increased tourist traffic through White River Junction would require hotels in the White Mountains, and they moved there to manage the different hotels that they had purchased.

## OSGOOD TRAIL

The Osgood Trail was cut in 1878 and is the oldest trail still in use to the summit of Mt. Madison. The trail leaves opposite the Glen House site and ascends the Osgood Ridge.

The trail was cleared by Ben F. Osgood, a famous guide at the Glen House during the late 1800's.

## PASSACONAWAY, MT.      Elevation 4,060

Mt. Passaconaway, named for Chief Passaconaway of the

Penacook Indians, is located south of the Kancamagus Highway in the Sandwich Range. (See Abenaki Ravine.)

## PASTURE PATH

The Pasture Path on Randolph Hill today passes through
deep woods that were once the open pastures and fields of the
farms on Randolph Hill. The path, originally cleared by Elliot
Torrey, extends from the eastern end of Randolph Hill to
Lookout Ledge.

## PEBOAMAUK FALL

This 60 foot moss covered waterfall is located at the eastern
end of the Ice Gulch. Peboamauk is the Abenaki word for
"Home of the Winter." These waterfalls are a two mile walk
from the Randolph Hill Road.

## PEABODY RIVER

The Peabody River flows north from Pinkham Notch, past
the Glen House site and into Gorham where it joins the
Androscoggin River.

The legend of the naming of this river is one of the unique
stories in the White Mountains. Reportedly, a Mr. Peabody, of
Andover, Massachusetts, was "present at the birth of the river."
Mr. Peabody claimed that he was spending the night in an Indian
cabin on Mt. Washington when he was awakened by a loud
noise. Mr. Peabody feared for his life and escaped from the cabin
just before a torrent of water sprang from out of the mountain
and swept the cabin away.

Any visitor to the White Mountains quickly realizes that this river has been here, in the bottom of this valley, for many thousands of years and that its formation did not occur suddenly in the middle of the night. Mr. Peabody may have either had a very fanciful imagination or a dream, or perhaps both.

## PEEK, WILLIAM H.

William H. Peek was one of the path builders who made his summer home at the Ravine House in Randolph. Peek came to Randolph for 25 summers after his first visit in 1878. In that year, after the death of his wife, Peek took a trip and discovered the White Mountains when his train stopped in Gorham. Peek used his own financial resources in his trail building projects over the quarter century that he visited Randolph. Today a glacial boulder, on the northern side of Route 2 west of the Randolph Hill Road, bears a plaque that commemorates Peek's contributions to the area.

## PEMIGEWASSET RIVER and
### Mt. Pemigewasset                    Elevation 2,554

The headwaters of the Pemigewasset River are between Mt. Liberty and Little Haystack Mountain in the Franconia Range. The river flows south out of the White Mountains and merges with the Baker River north of Plymouth and then with the Merrimack River in Franklin, New Hampshire.

Mt. Pemigewasset is located at the southern end of Franconia Notch across from the Flume. The "Indian Head" profile is on the southern face of this mountain.

Pemigewasset is an Abenaki word meaning "Rapidly Moving."

**PICKERING, MT.**                    Elevation 1,942

This mountain is located north of Route 302, about three miles west of Glen (Bartlett), New Hampshire, and honors the Pickering family, early explorers of the White Mountains. Charles Pickering, a zoologist, first climbed Mt. Washington with his friend William Oakes in 1826. For many years after that Pickering continued to explore the White Mountains. One of Pickering's nephews, Edward Charles Pickering, a Professor of Physics at MIT, would become the first President of the Appalachian Mountain Club when it was formed in 1876.

**PIERCE, MT.** (See Mt. Clinton)        Elevation 4,312

Mt. Pierce is named after New Hampshire's only United States President, Franklin Pierce. Pierce was President from 1853 to 1857. During this period, he developed a friendship with Jefferson Davis, who would later be President of the Confederacy. This friendship with Davis and the south may have alienated Pierce from the citizens of New Hampshire.

The name "Mt. Clinton" is more commonly associated with this mountain.

**PILOT RANGE and Mt. Pilot**         Elevation 3,710

The Pilot Range lies north of the town of Jefferson and includes parts of Jefferson, Stark, Kilkenny, and Randolph. Mt. Pilot was originally called Little Moosehillock. This area is almost as wild and remote today as it was in the last century. In Sweetser's guide, the area is described as "never thoroughly explored."

There are two stories about the derivation of the name "Pilot" for this mountain and range. One story says that these hills served to guide hunters from the mountain areas to the Connecticut River valley. Thus they were called the "land pilot hills."

A more romantic story says that a hunter, Jonathan Willard, would often go hunting and trapping in these hills for extended periods of time. On one occasion he became lost. Exhausted, he followed his dog back to the hunting camp. After this experience the dog was named "Pilot," and the mountain and the range were named after him.

## PINKHAM NOTCH

In early literature Pinkham Notch is referred to as both the "Eastern Pass" and "The Glen." In addition to Franconia Notch and Crawford Notch, this is one of the three mountain passes in northern New Hampshire.

A road was first cut through this notch by Captain John Evans (Evans Notch) in 1774. However, after the incorporation of the town of Randolph in 1824 the New Hampshire legislature contracted with Daniel Pinkham to expand the then existing road. Daniel Pinkham was the son of Joseph Pinkham, an early settler in Jackson. Daniel Pinkham was also a farmer, a blacksmith, a dentist, a mason, a carpenter and a Baptist preacher. To honor Daniel Pinkham, the notch was named after him.

Today Route 16 passes through the notch, and the AMC Pinkham Notch camp, the regional headquarters for the AMC, is located here.

## POND OF SAFETY

The Pond of Safety is located at the northern edge of the town of Randolph, behind Mt. Crescent and between the Pliny Mountains and Randolph.

During the American Revolution this pond served as a sanctuary for four American soldiers, Benjamin Hicks, James Ryder, William Danforth, and Lazarus Holmes, who had been captured and then released by the British army. As a condition of their parole they agreed not to return to fighting. However, upon returning to the American army they were asked to take up arms. Fearing arrest for failing to follow these orders, and not wanting to violate the terms of their parole, they fled to northern New Hampshire where they lived as hermits and found safety by this isolated pond. After the Revolution was over they were exonerated of the charges of desertion, and they received their military pensions. Several of these soldiers settled in the town of Jefferson.

## PRESIDENTIAL RANGE

The Presidential Range refers to Mt. Washington, elevation, 6,288 feet, Mt. Adams, elevation 5,798 feet, Mt. Jefferson, elevation 5,715 feet and Mt. Madison, elevation 5,363 feet. (See entries for these mountains.)

Mt. Washington was named in 1784 by Dr. Jeremy Belknap, the historian of New Hampshire, when he visited, climbed, and explored the mountain. The other peaks remained un-named until 1820 when a group of men from Lancaster, New Hampshire, led by Ethan Allen Crawford, climbed Mt. Washington and gave names to the surrounding peaks. One prominent member of this group was John W. Weeks, the son of Captain Weeks who had settled in Lancaster in 1786. A second member of the group was Philip Carrigain, who had served as New Hampshire's Secretary of State and after whom Mt. Carrigain is named.

## PROFILE MT.

While Mounts Washington, Adams, Jefferson, and Madison are named after the first four persons to become American Presidents, Mt. Clay, between Mt. Washington and Mt. Jefferson is named after Henry Clay. Clay was a statesman who possessed a great deal of Presidential ambition but who never achieved that office. Mt. Clay was not named by the group from Lancaster, but later by William Oakes.

Writing in *The White Hills*, the Reverend Starr King deplored the new names:

> What a pity that the hills could not have kept the names which the Indian tribes gave to them... Webster, Clinton, Pleasant, Franklin, Monroe, Washington, Clay, Jefferson, Adams, Madison. What a wretched jumble. These are what we have taken in exchange for such Indian words as Agiocochook, which is the baptismal title of Mt. Washington.

There are many above treeline hiking trails between Mt. Madison and Mt. Washington. When King wrote about his first trip across these peaks, he concluded that "the only trouble with the route is that there is too much to see in one day."

There are other mountains in northern New Hampshire named after other Presidents—Lincoln, Garfield, and Cleveland. However, these mountains are not commonly thought of as being in the "Presidential Range."

## PROFILE MOUNTAIN (See Cannon Mountain and Franconia)

## RAILROADS IN THE WHITE MOUNTAINS

There are four kinds of railroads that have a history in the

White Mountains. The Cog Railway to the summit of Mt. Washington is described earlier. The development of freight and passenger railroads brought commerce and tourism to northern New Hampshire. A fourth railroad system that has disappeared even further into the history books are the logging railroads that were of vital importance to that industry in the late 19th century.

## Logging Railroads

At the height of the logging industry, there were 17 logging railroads that climbed into the hills and valleys of the White Mountains. The development of these railroads did not come until after the civil war, during which time, the full potential of the railroad was recognized for industrial purposes. After the Civil War the state of New Hampshire sold off its large holdings of land in the White Mountains. Lumber companies purchased these tracts of land and then proceeded to exploit the forests that were there. In 1907 it was reported that 650 million board feet of lumber were cut in these virgin forests.

The logging railroads brought the lumber out of the forests to the larger commercial railroads that took it to the cities of the northeast. At first the logging railroads were narrow gauge, but this was later changed to the standard gauge so that they could more easily connect with the commercial freight lines. In constructing the logging railroads in the mountains, railroad ties were made from the native fir and hemlock. Since these were not treated with preservatives, it is possible to find remaining evidence of them in only a few places. When they were active, the wood burning steam railroads operated primarily during the winter months when there was a frozen railroad bed.

The standard industry practice was to cut everything that stood in the forest, remove the desired lumber, and leave the

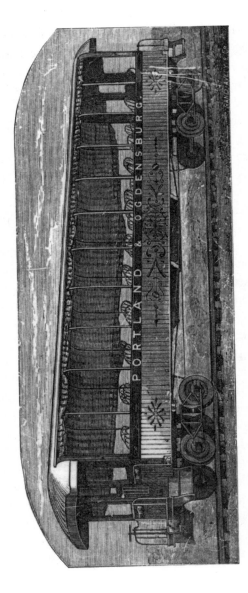

remaining slash to dry on the ground. This dried slash was to later become the fuel for vast forest fires that left permanent scars in the White Mountains. In 1903, the fires in the Kilkenny area destroyed an estimated 25,110 acres creating a vast charred wasteland. It is reported that during 1903, a total of 80,000 acres of forest were burned in the White Mountains, fueled by the slash left behind by loggers. Nature has asserted its power and reclaimed the mountains for the forest that is enjoyed today.

When the virgin forests of the White Mountains were cut at the end of the last century "forestry" was not the developed ecological science that we know today. Only one logging company was operated by a far sighted family that practiced selective cutting. The Saunders family of Lawrence and Lowell, Massachusetts, owned the eight mile Sawyer River Railroad at the southern end of Crawford Notch. The forestry practices employed by this company enabled it to have several cuttings.

Another company developed portable camps in order to reduce its costs. J. E. Henry & Sons built its logging camps of boards rather than logs. These logging camps could be taken apart and moved to different sites at significant savings to the company.

It has been written that the logging company presidents considered themselves also to be presidents of railroad companies. One "Railroad President," J. E. Brown, discovered that by sending a complimentary pass to other railroad presidents, he in turn would receive a similar pass enabling him to travel in style and comfort around the country on other railroads. This reportedly

---

*Portland and Ogdensburg Railroad Observation Car. Chisholm's White Mountain Guide*, 1880. From the author's collection.

worked very well until the President of the Pennsylvania Railroad arrived and presented his pass to ride on Brown's railroad. He was neither amused nor entertained by his ride on an open flat car that lurched along the uneven tracks through the forest.

## Passenger Railroads

America's prosperity after the Civil War allowed many people to look for places where they could easily spend their vacations. When the White Mountains of New Hampshire became their destination, the railway companies responded to the need for increased passenger service by expanding their services to this region. Eastman's 1878 guide describes how a traveler could leave Boston in the morning and arrive at the summit of Mt. Washington for the sunset with only one change of trains at the base station of the Cog Railway (photo page 36).

White River Junction, Vermont, became a busy railway center for visitors coming from New York. There was considerable confusion here as eight different railways converged on this transfer point. From here passengers would continue up the Connecticut River Valley to St. Johnsbury, Vermont, and then east into the White Mountains.

The Boston, Concord and Montreal Railway had *The White Mountain Express*. This train often carried 12 to 16 sleeper cars from southern New England which were "dropped off" during the night at hotels in Whitefield, Jefferson, Bethlehem, and Fabyan. From Bethlehem there was a narrow gauge line, The Profile and Franconia Notch Railroad Company, that continued to the Profile House. This entire railway company consisted of two steam engines, the *Profile* and the *Echo*, two passenger cars and two baggage cars (see page 93).

In addition to the increased passenger service, different

railways had open observation cars for tourists. The Portland and Ogdensburg line had a such an observation car which ran through Crawford Notch over the Frankenstein Trestle (see pages 73 and 136).

## RANDOLPH PATH

The Randolph Path, built between 1893 and 1899 by J. Rayner Edmands, goes from the location of the old railway station in East Randolph on the Dolly Copp Road to Edmands Col where it joins with the Gulfside Trail. This trail traverses much of Mt. Adams and connects with many of the other trails on the mountain. (See Edmands Col and Edmands Path.)

There was a certain competition between the early path builders. The Rev. Joseph Torrey, a summer visitor in Randolph, had planned to build a path from the railway station to Mt. Adams when he discovered that Edmands was already undertaking such a project. Torrey remarked to his son that Edmands had saved him a lot of work.

## RANDOLPH, TOWN OF

Randolph, a "cold and rugged township," is located at the base of the northern Presidentials, Mt. Madison and Mt. Adams. There are many trailheads in Randolph, the largest and most often used is known today as "Appalachia" on Route 2.

Randolph was first known as "Durand," after John Durand of London to whom the area was granted in 1772. The first settlers came to Randolph in 1824. When "Durand" was incorporated, it was given its present name after the statesman and orator John Randolph of Virginia, a descendant of Pocahontas.

Randolph has long had a summer community and at one time

the town contained three hotels—the Ravine House, the Mt. Crescent House, and the Mountain View House, once known as the Kelsey Cottage. These inns and the surrounding cottages became the summer headquarters for the path building that occurred in this region. It was here in Randolph that summer residents and path builders such as J. Rayner Edmands, Charles Torrey, E. B. Cook, George Sargent, William H. Peek, Louis F. Cutter, E. J. Hincks, and William Grey Nowell would meet with some of Randolph's permanent residents such as Charles E. Lowe, Hubbard Hunt, and Laban Watson to plan and work on the opening of the forests to hikers. Through the efforts of the Randolph Mountain Club this work continues today.

During a visit to the White Mountains, the Reverend Starr King once spoke with a Randolph farmer. After the farmer had expressed his wish that the mountains could be flat, King responded, "But the great summits must look peculiarly grand in winter." The farmer quietly responded, "Guess not, it's too 'tarnal cold. You come and see the same clouds whirling round them peaks three weeks at a time, and you's wish the hills was moved off and dumped somewhere else."

In 1943 Randolph found itself placed in the record books when the largest twenty-four hour snowfall in the United States was recorded there. Between November 22nd and November 23rd, 56 inches (4 feet, 8 inches) of snow fell in a single storm on Randolph Hill.

The Randolph Church, built between 1883 and 1884, is located on the northern side of Route 2 east of the Randolph Hill Road. Today the church is used primarily for summer services.

---

*The Mount Crescent House, Randolph, New Hampshire.* Photo by Guy Shorey. New Hampshire Historical Society Collection.

## RAYMOND PATH

During the 1870's, a Major Curtis B. Raymond of Boston was a frequent summer guest at the Glen House. During this period Raymond re-opened a trail that had been previously cleared by J. M. Thompson, the proprietor of the Glen House. This path became known as the Raymond path into Tuckerman Ravine. After spending years at the Glen House, Raymond spent several summers in Crawford Notch working on paths in that region.

## RESOLUTION, MT.                    Elevation 3,428

Located north of Mt. Crawford on the Montalban Ridge is Mt. Resolution, named by Dr. Samuel Bemis. Bemis used this name in recognition of the determination of Nathaniel T. P. Davis to clear a trail to the summit of Mt. Washington. Davis, married to Abel Crawford's daughter Hannah, first started a trail up this mountain in 1845. He became discouraged and stopped his project. He later returned and completed it.

## RIPLEY FALLS

Located on Avalanche Brook behind the Willey House Station in Crawford Notch are the Ripley Falls. The Rev. Starr King named these falls after a friend Henry Wheelock Ripley who visited the White Mountains for many years.

## ROSEBROOK RANGE and
## Mt. Rosebrook                    Elevation 3,007

The Rosebrook Range rises to the west above the area known as Fabyan, near Crawford Notch in the town of Carroll.

This range and mountain are named after Eleazar Rosebrook, who was born in Grafton, Massachusetts, in 1747. After marrying in 1772, Rosebrook moved north to Vermont. After living in Lunenburg, Vermont, Rosebrook moved to Colebrook, New Hampshire, where he lived 30 miles from his nearest neighbor. At the time of the American Revolution, Rosebrook moved to Guildhall, Vermont, as protection for his family. During the Revolution, Rosebrook served as a spy for the American army. In 1790, Rosebrook's daughter Hannah married Abel Crawford.

After the marriage, Crawford left his wife with her parents and went to find a home for his family in the White Mountains. On this trip Crawford settled on land near the site known today as "Fabyan." After several years, Rosebrook purchased this farm from his son-in-law. Rosebrook enlarged the inn and renamed it the "Old Red Tavern." Crawford and his family moved further into the notch that now bears his family name. Rosebrook built a sawmill and ran his house as an inn. He died of cancer on his farm in 1817 at the age of 70.

In the early 1900's there was a small cluster of trails in the Rosebrook Range that served the guests of the local hotels. This network of trails was abandoned when the hotels closed.

## ROYCE, MT.                           Elevation 3,202

Located above and to the west of Evans Notch is Mt. Royce, named after Captain Vere Royce, a surveyor and pre-revolutionary war soldier. Around 1770 Royce had been one of the two people who received a grant to what is now the town of Bartlett. Neither Royce nor his partner ever settled that grant.

## SARGENT CLIFF and Sargent Path

Named for George A. Sargent, the Sargent Cliff is up the sides of the Ice Gulch, on Mt. Crescent. The Sargent Path, from the Durand Road in Randolph up to Lookout Ledge, is also named for him. Sargent first visited Randolph in 1882 and then returned regularly until his death there in 1932. Sargent was a physician who graduated from the Harvard Medical School in 1888.

## SAUNDERS, MT.                                    Elevation 3,120

Mt. Saunders is located south of Mt. Nancy and above Notchland in Crawford Notch. There are no trails on this mountain.

This mountain is named after Daniel Saunders of the Saunders family of Lawrence and Lowell, Massachusetts. Another member of the family, Charles Saunders was a charter member of the AMC. This family owned a logging company and a small logging railway in the White Mountains. Their company was the only one that employed any enlightened "forestry" practices in its work. Between 1875 and 1878 there were legal disputes over the ownership of land between the Bartlett Land and Lumber Company and Daniel Saunders. These disputes resulted in a U. S. Supreme Court case. The legal briefs that were filed with the court described the "wild tracts of land in New Hampshire" as "rough country to travel over; a pretty rough country to survey; that the country was wooded, rough with rocks, ledges and swamps."

---

*The Shelburne Birches.* Photo by Guy Shorey. The New Hampshire Historical Society Collection.

The
SHELBURNE BIRCHES
ACQUIRED BY THE TOWN
AS A TRIBUTE TO ITS
CITIZENS IN THE SERVICE
OF OUR COUNTRY

## SAWYER POND and Sawyer River

This river enters the Saco River between Bartlett and Notchland. Both the river and pond are named after Benjamin Sawyer who, with Timothy Nash, brought a horse through Crawford Notch and thereby proved that it would be possible to build a road there. Sawyer Pond has also been called Bemis Lake.

This pond has been described as "the usual New Hampshire mountain lake, a few acres in area, boggy and marshy and thick all around with a tangle of tough alders."

## SHELBURNE, TOWN OF

The town of Shelburne was incorporated in 1769 and named after the English Earl of Shelburne, William Petty Fitzmaurice. Shelburne, located to the east of Gorham, was settled two years after it was incorporated. The Androscoggin River flows through the center of the town.

In 1890 a guidebook stated:

> There is no village of Shelburne. A post office, a Union Church, a sawmill, a small summer hotel, a few farm-houses, white amid the universal green of meadow and forest, one or two gentlemen's summer houses, make the hamlet and the rest is given over to nature; and, if the wishes of the most intelligent of the Shelburne people prevail, this is as far as modern civilization will ever be allowed to come.... They have nearly all of the blessings of civilization with few of its drawbacks.

The Philbrook Farm Inn in Shelburne was founded by Harvey Philbrook who settled in Shelburne in 1835. Philbrook moved to the present farm in 1860 and soon after that began to take in a few guests. Over the years, the inn has been expanded by Philbrook's descendants. It is now reported to be the oldest hotel in the United States that has been operated continuously by the same family.

Today U. S. Route 2 passes through the "Shelburne Memorial Birches," a memorial grove of birch trees dedicated to the soldiers from Shelburne who served in World War II.

## SHORT LINE TRAIL

The Short Line Trail, at the bottom of King Ravine, connects the Airline Trail with the King Ravine Trail. This trail was cleared between 1899 and 1901 by J. Rayner Edmands.

## SIX HUSBAND TRAIL

There is a story of a queen of the Penacook Indians, Weetamoo, who had six husbands. This trail up Mt. Jefferson from the Great Gulf is named for them. Weetamoo Falls in the Great Gulf is named after the Queen. The Wamsutta Trail is named for the first of the six husbands.

## SNYDER BROOK

This brook, in the valley between Durand Ridge and Gordon Ridge, was reportedly named by Dr. William Nowell after a dog named "Snyder" that belonged to Charles E. Lowe. Philip Ayres of the Society for the Protection of New Hampshire Forests described this brook as "a thousand little falls that gurgle in the ear long after the scene has changed."

## SOCIETY FOR THE PROTECTION OF NEW HAMPSHIRE FORESTS (SPNHF)

Few visitors to the White Mountains are aware of and recognize the importance of this Concord, New Hampshire,

environmental organization, known as the "Society," in the creation and establishment of the White Mountain National Forest, Franconia Notch State Forest and Crawford Notch State Forest. Today's visitors are much indebted to this organization, its founders, and its dedicated employees and members.

The SPNHF was founded in 1901 by a group of prominent men from New Hampshire and Boston. One name recognizable today by anybody familiar with Boston is James Jackson Storrow, the man who was responsible for building the Charles River Basin and after whom Storrow Drive is named. Storrow was the second treasurer for the Society and his son succeeded him in that capacity.

The Society's initial concern was with the uncontrolled cutting of New Hampshire's forests and the subsequent effects that this was having on the streams and wildlife of northern New Hampshire.

It was not until 1911, when with the assistance of John W. Weeks, a Massachusetts Congressman who had been born in Lancaster, New Hampshire, that legislation was passed creating what would eventually become the White Mountain National Forest (WMNF). The 1911 Weeks Act was very general and provided that lands could be acquired to protect the navigability of streams anywhere in the U. S. It took imagination and creativity to extend this to the streams of northern New Hampshire, but that is what the Society did.

Philip Ayres was the first forester employed by the Society. Ayres had previously worked in the administration of charities

---

*Giant's Stairs from Thorn Hill.* Samuel A. Drake.
From the author's collection.

but at the age of 40, sought a career change and took a number of forestry courses. His knowledge of forestry and his administrative experience led to the Society in 1902 where he worked until his retirement in 1935. During this period the Weeks Act establishing the WMNF was passed and Ayres was to see both the size of the WMNF grow and the work of the Society expanded. In 1909, before the passage of the Weeks Act, Ayres wrote of New Hampshire's forests:

> There has been a reckless waste of the vast forest wealth of the nation, which is still going on, but changes for the better are being made in important directions.... Forests may and should be so managed that they will become profitable and yield permanent revenues; but this occurs usually only after long periods of good management. The great need in the White Mountains is for timely action, since the forest waste now going on can be repaired only at a very great cost.

In later years, when logging companies threatened to purchase Franconia Notch, it was Ayres who organized the fund raising that resulted in the present state park.

Upon Ayres' retirement, the Dean of the Yale School of Forestry, Henry Solon Graves, said to him: "You did more than anyone else to bring about the passage of the Weeks law that is one of the epoch-making measures of forest history. You made the White Mountain National Forest possible. It stands as a monument to your creative efforts."

Ayres himself wrote about the trail systems that had been created "to the most interesting places" in the White Mountains.

---

*Presidential Range from Bretton Woods.* Photo by Eugene S. Jones. New Hampshire Historical Society Collection.

Ayres additionally recognized the contributions of the individuals and organizations that had built and maintained these systems.

Former New Hampshire Governor Sherman Adams, after whom the new building at the summit of Mt. Washington is named, wrote of the Society:

> But you cannot talk about forest history in New Hampshire without acknowledging that for most of the principal conservation projects, for reforms in government's approach to wilderness and timberland, and for most of the public acquisitions of places of great natural beauty, we have the Society to thank. It is largely through the efforts of this organization that much of the natural heritage and the environmental values of this state have been preserved. New Hampshire still needs the Society and its activists and revolutionaries.

For additional information about this organization, the address is: 54 Portsmouth Street Concord, NH 03301-5400.

## SPAULDING LAKE

This little lake, at the bottom of the Great Gulf and visible from the edge of the gulf, is named for John H. Spaulding, the author of *Historical Relics of the White Mountains*, the first combination guide and history of the White Mountains that was published in 1855. Spaulding first visited this lake in 1853. At one time he was the manager of the Tip Top House on the summit of Mt. Washington. In the guidebook, Spaulding noted that "J.H.S. 1853" was carved into a stone near the lake. Spaulding called attention to the lake by writing: "The Gulf of Mexico (The Great Gulf) and Spaulding's Lake are at least worth a trip from the Atlantic, for all who would look with proud satisfaction upon nature in her sublimest mood."

## SPAULDING SPRING

This spring, located in Edmands Col, was named after the Reverend Henry G. Spaulding of Brookline, Massachusetts. The spring was given this name by Charles E. Lowe and Dr. William Nowell.

## SPUR

A spur is a small or minor summit that projects from a larger one. It is not really a separate mountain. Examples of this are Boott Spur, which is called a spur, and Mt. Willard, which is really a spur of Mt. Field.

## STAIRS MOUNTAIN                    Elevation 3,460

Stairs Mountain is located on the eastern side of Crawford Notch and may be climbed via the Davis Path.

The ridge on the southern end of the mountain, appears to be stairs for giants which are visible from many locations throughout the notch. Dr. Samuel Bemis named both Giant Stairs and Stairs Mountain (see page 148).

## STICKNEY, MT.                      Elevation 2,570

Mt. Stickney rises over the Mount Washington Hotel at Bretton Woods to the west of Route 302. The Stickney Memorial Chapel is a small church located on Route 302 just south of the entrance to the hotel.

Joseph Stickney was a wealthy New York businessman who became closely associated with two White Mountain hotels. In

## SUCCESS, MT.

1881 Stickney purchased the Mt. Pleasant House and then proceeded to make improvements to the building including the installation of a well, private baths, and electricity. This hotel was torn down in 1939. Stickney's more lasting contribution was the Mount Washington Hotel at Bretton Woods which he built in 1902. Today this hotel is the last of the large hotels in the White Mountains.

### SUCCESS, MT.                  Elevation 3,590

Mt. Success, in the Mahoosuc Range, is named after the township in which it is located, Success, New Hampshire. The township was granted in 1773. This was the same year that the colonists refused to allow the importation of tea into Boston and that the Stamp Act was repealed. It has been suggested that the "Success" of one or both of those historical events is the origin of the name. The town of Success was never widely populated.

### THOMPSON FALLS

These falls are located on a stream to the east of Route 16 and just north of the Wildcat Mountain Ski area in Pinkham Notch. These falls are named in honor of J. M. Thompson, the proprietor of the first Glen House. In October 1869, after a severe rain, Thompson drowned in the Peabody River.

### THOREAU FALLS

At the southern end of Zealand Notch are the Thoreau Falls, named after Henry David Thoreau, writer, naturalist, and

---

*Travelers in a storm, Mount Washington.* Samuel A. Drake. From the author's collection.

philosopher, who first visited the White Mountains in 1839 and returned for a second visit in 1858.

## TIN MOUNTAIN                                 Elevation 2,020
Located to the east of the village of Jackson, Tin Mountain was the site of the first tin mines in the United States. Minerals are no longer mined here nor at other sites throughout the White Mountains whose names suggest ores and mineral deposits.

## TOM, MT.                                      Elevation 4,047
Mt. Tom is located above and to the west of Crawford Notch. This mountain is named after Thomas Crawford, the son of Abel Crawford, who for many years managed the hotel that was located in the notch. This mountain was named by Charles Hitchcock.

## TUCKERMAN RAVINE
Located on the eastern-side of Mt. Washington, Tuckerman Ravine is a classic example of a glacial cirque. This ravine is easily accessible to hikers from Pinkham Notch. The Tuckerman Ravine trail is the shortest hiking trail to the summit of Mt. Washington. During the spring months, and often into early summer, "Tuckerman's," as it is fondly known, becomes the last place where skiing can be found in the east. The Inferno Race was a ski race from the top of the Tuckerman's Headwall to Pinkham Notch which has been discontinued for reasons of safety. The 1939 record of 6 minutes and 29 seconds was never

---

*Spring Skiing in Tuckerman Ravine.* Postcard from the New Hampshire Historical Society Collection.

broken. To experience this rite of spring skiing, skiers must carry all of their equipment up into "the bowl."

This ravine is named in honor of Dr. Edward Tuckerman, Professor of Botany at Amherst College from 1858 to 1886. After Professor Tuckerman's first visit to the White Mountains in 1837, he returned frequently to study and collect specimens of the vegetation of the White Mountains. One of his greatest contributions was to characterize the vegetation of the Presidential Range into four distinct categories: 1) The Lower Forest, 2) The Upper Forest, 3) The Sub Alpine Zone and 4) the Alpine Zone.

Tuckerman contributed two chapters to Starr King's *The White Hills* published in 1871. One of these chapters, entitled "The Vegetation of the White Mountains," describes his botanical findings and the early research and findings of other scientists. Tuckerman is credited with having named Oakes Gulf after that botanist.

## VALLEY WAY

The Valley Way Trail ascends Mt. Madison beginning at the Appalachia parking area on Route 2 in Randolph. The path was first cleared by Laban Watson and E. B. Cook. When Edmands did his work on this path, he used parts of the original trail and relocated other areas to conform with his idea of following the contours of the mountain. The trail closely follows Snyder Brook.

## WAMSUTTA TRAIL

This trail ascends the Chandler Ridge from the Great Gulf

---

*The summit of Mt. Washington in winter.* Stereoscopic view. New Hampshire Historical Society Collection.

159

Trail. Wamsutta, the son of Massasoit, a friend of the early Pilgrims, was the first of the six husbands of Queen Weetamoo of the Penacook Indians. Wamsutta is the only one of the husbands individually remembered in the White Mountains. (See Six Husbands Trail.)

**WASHINGTON, MT.** (See Agiocochook)          Elevation 6,288

Mt. Washington is the highest point east of the Mississippi and North of the Carolina's. It was reportedly first seen from the ocean in 1524 by Giovanni da Verrazano from off of Portsmouth, New Hampshire. The Native Americans considered Mt. Washington to be the home of the gods and did not climb it. Darby Field first climbed to its summit in 1642. Today many visitors ascend the summit via the Auto Road, the Cog Railway, or by hiking the many trails that surround the mountain.

The summit once included a hotel, but no overnight accommodations are available now. Today the summit includes broadcast towers for television and radio stations, the Mount Washington Weather Observatory, and the Mount Washington State Park.

The visitor to the summit, via the Cog Railway, the auto road, or hiking trails, should be prepared for extremes of weather. The combination of wind and cold found here gives Mt. Washington the distinction of having the worst recorded weather in the world. In April 1934 the Weather Observatory recorded the highest wind ever recorded on earth, 231 miles per hour. On February 12, 1967, the observatory simultaneously

---

*Old Summit House, Mt. Washington.* Photo by Eugene S. Jones. New Hampshire Historical Society Collection.

recorded a temperature of -41 degrees Fahrenheit and a wind of 110 miles per hour. The chill factor for this combination of wind and cold was not on the charts.

Mt. Washington can be a cold and inhospitable place even in the middle of the summer. Gusts of over 100 miles per hour have been recorded here in all months of the year. It is rare to have a windless day on the summit where the average windspeed is 35 miles per hour. A hurricane wind is 75 miles per hour and that wind speed is exceeded on over 100 days per year. The record high temperature on the summit is only 72° F, recorded in 1975; while the record low temperature is -47° F, recorded in January 1934. The average temperature is only 26.9° F. The temperature has been known to drop as quickly as 1 degree Fahrenheit per minute for half an hour or more. The warmest month of the year is July, with an average temperature of 49° F. Snow has been recorded on the summit in every month. During the winter, the average snowfall is 195 inches. The average annual precipitation is 73½ inches. Sleet and snow storms are so frequent on Mt. Washington that the U. S. Air Force once constructed a facility here to test its equipment.

The earliest guide books recommended taking extra clothing to the summit in all months of the year. The 1863 Eastman guide described the hotel guests one mid-summer day as follows: "Around these fires (wood stoves) the shivering guests crowd, and present about the same appearance as travelers in January stopping to warm themselves at a country inn." Chisholm wrote in 1880 about the need for "overcoats and shawls" even in August.

The headquarters of the Mount Washington State Park is the Sherman Adams Visitors Center. This building is named in honor of the former lumber company president, Congressman, Governor of New Hampshire, Special Assistant to President Eisenhower, and President of Loon Mountain Corporation. The building, dedicated in 1980, replaced the former Summit House and Observatory which have been removed. The Adams building contains the Mt. Washington Observatory, a gift shop, cafeteria, and information about Mt. Washington and the White Mountains.

Adams was a long time friend of the White Mountains. As a student at Dartmouth College, he was a member of the AMC trail crews. In 1920, after getting into top physical condition, he hiked the 83 miles from Skyline Cabin, just north of Franconia Notch to Hanover, New Hampshire, in one day. This hike had a vertical rise of 5,600 feet and a descent of 6,500 feet. While the distance record had been subsequently broken, the combination of distance and vertical rise and fall has never been matched. In later years, Adams was the Woodlands Manager for the Parker-Young Co., a large lumber company in Lincoln. At the same time, he was on the Executive Committee of the Society for the Protection of New Hampshire Forests which was actively working on environmental concerns and the creation of the White Mountain National Forest. Adams' lifetime interest in the White Mountains, Mt. Washington, and the State of New Hampshire make it appropriate that this visitor's center be named in his honor.

From the summit of Mt. Washington it is possible to see into five states—New Hampshire, Maine, Vermont, New York and Massachusetts, and Canada. On a clear day it is possible to see the Atlantic Ocean. After spending the night on the summit,

P. T. Barnum is reported to have said of the view, "This is the second greatest show on earth." Modern pollution is today responsible for the deterioration of that view.

The Reverend Starr King described Mt. Washington as follows:

> ...the sovereign dome of New England, but it is very difficult to make him behave as such. In the Glen, (near the Glen House site) Mount Adams looks higher and more proud. Seen from North Conway, he is not isolated from the rest of the range, and wears no grandeur about the summit. At Lancaster he looks humpbacked. In Shelburne he appears heavy and dowdy. From Bethlehem he shows grand height, but unsatisfactory form. The village of Jefferson, on the Cherry Mountain road, about thirteen miles from Gorham, furnishes the best position for studying his lines and height in connection with the rest of the range, But Mount Hayes is the chair set by the Creator at the proper distance and angle to appreciate and enjoy his kingly prominence.

## WATERVILLE VALLEY

Located north of Plymouth and east of Interstate 93 is Waterville Valley, one of the popular summer resorts in the mountains. This region was not "discovered" until 1819, and it was not incorporated until 1829. The summer resort that flourished here owes its development to Nathaniel Greeley, the innkeeper who built both walking trails and bridle paths for his guests. Greeley's trails became the first trail system in the northeast. One of the bridle paths connected with trails near Crawford Notch. Greeley's inn, built in 1860, burned in 1967 at the time that the modern ski resort was developed. His name is today remembered at Greeley Ponds, north of Waterville Valley.

Surrounding Waterville Valley are several peaks bearing Native American names that appear to be out of place in New Hampshire. Mt. Tecumseh is named after Tecumseh, a Shawnee Chief from Ohio. Mt. Osceola is named after a Seminole Chief in Florida. There are varying and contradictory stories about how these names came to these mountains. However, as with all of the other locations that bear Native American names, these names were given by the white man. To the east of Waterville Valley is Mt. Tripyramid, easily identified by its three distinctive peaks. To the south of Waterville Valley is the Acteon Ridge, named in honor of the last Chief of the Pemigewassets in New Hampshire.

## WATSON PATH

Cleared in 1882, the Watson Path to the summit of Mt. Madison from Randolph was one of many trails that was cleared by Laban Watson. He began clearing trails in 1880 at the age of 30.

Watson was interested in clearing trails in part because he was the proprietor of the Ravine House, a large hotel in Randolph used by many of the early hikers. The Ravine House was used as the base for Louis F. Cutter, whose mapwork is still sold by the AMC and for path builders such as Edmands, Cook, Nowell and Peek. The late 19th century was an important path building era in the history of the White Mountains and it was around the fireplaces of the Ravine House that many plans and findings were discussed. For these path builders, the work had three distinct stages: First the dreams of having a path in a specific place; Then, prospecting for a route—scouting, climbing trees for views, shouting to co-workers and blazing the path; Lastly, the job of building the path.

In 1909, Watson sold his hotel and retired to nearby

Coldbrook Lodge. After Route 2 was paved and widened in 1927, the increased noise resulted in fewer guests staying for the lengthy periods of time that had been common before. The Ravine House was closed in 1960 and its contents were auctioned in 1962. Today the site is owned by the Town of Randolph and the Randolph Foundation.

### WAUMBEK, MT.                                    Elevation 4,020

Rising above the town of Jefferson is Mt. Waumbek. This is the Abenaki word for "white," therefore, "White Mountain." Leading from the town of Jefferson there is a trail ascending Mt. Starr King and Mt. Waumbek.

### WEBSTER, MT.                                    Elevation 3,910
### Webster Cliffs, The Daniel Webster Trail and
### The Daniel Webster Scout Trail

This mountain, the cliffs and the trails are named for the American statesman, Daniel Webster. Webster was born in Salisbury, New Hampshire, and attended Dartmouth College. He practiced law in New Hampshire before moving to Boston to be a lawyer there. After visiting the summit of Mt. Washington in the summer of 1831, Webster wrote of the "cold reception" that he had received there. With his guide, Ethan Allen Crawford, they had snow squalls as they returned from the summit to Crawford Notch.

Mt. Webster is located on the eastern side of Crawford Notch and south of Mt. Jackson. The Webster-Jackson Trail starts in

---

*The Ravine House, Randolph, New Hampshire.* Photo by Guy Shorey. New Hampshire Historical Society Collection.

Crawford Notch near Saco Lake. The Webster Cliff Trail branches off from this trail. Prior to being named Mt. Webster, this was known as "Notch Mountain."

The Daniel Webster Scout Trail, cleared by the Boy Scouts in 1933, ascends Mt. Madison from the Dolly Copp Campground north of Pinkham Notch.

**WEEKS, MT.**                                        Elevation 3,890

Mt. Weeks in the Pliny Range north of Lancaster, New Hampshire, honors a family of early settlers and statesmen. The Reverend John Wingate Weeks was one of the early settlers of Lancaster. Another member of the family was a member of the group of Lancastrians who climbed Mt. Washington in 1820 and named the surrounding peaks. John W. Weeks, born in Lancaster in 1860, had an important role in the creation of the present day White Mountain National Forest. Weeks, a graduate of the U. S. Naval Academy, became a Boston businessman, a founder of the brokerage firm of Hornblower & Weeks, later a Congressman, then Senator, and then Secretary of War under Presidents Harding and Coolidge. As a Congressman, he was appointed to the Agricultural Committee where he sponsored the Weeks Act which resulted in the creation of the White Mountain National Forest. Some politicians wanted to nominate Weeks for President in 1916.

In response to his resignation as Secretary of War, President Coolidge wrote: "Perhaps no more valuable suggestion was made to the Congress during the war than the proposal you made for preparing for peace. It will remain, with the law for national forests, which bears your name, as a tribute to your statesmanship." After his death in 1926, the Weeks Bridge, between Cambridge and Boston, was dedicated in his memory. A son of John W. Weeks, Sinclair Weeks, represented Massachusetts in the U. S. Senate and was Secretary of Commerce under President Eisenhower.

## WEETAMOO FALLS

Located in the Great Gulf, Weetamoo Falls is named after a Queen of the Penacook Indians. Weetamoo died in 1676. (See Six Husbands Trail and Wamsutta Trail.)

## WESTSIDE TRAIL

This short trail, named for its location on the western side of the summit of Mt. Washington, connects the Gulfside Trail with the Crawford Path. Constructed in part by J. Rayner Edmands, the trail allows hikers to avoid crossing over the summit of Mt. Washington.

## WHITE HORSE LEDGE

The White Horse Ledge is above Echo Lake in North Conway. Trails lead up to this ledge from the Echo Lake State Park.

In his guide to the White Mountains, Sweetser writes that this ledge gets its name from the "fancied resemblance of a light colored spot on its front to a white horse dashing up a cliff." According to old New England folklore, if after seeing a white horse, a marriageable lady counted to 100, then the first gentlemen that she met would be her husband. This legend has contributed to the popularity of the ledge.

## WHITE MOUNTAIN NATIONAL FOREST (WMNF)

The White Mountain National Forest, WMNF, is within a

days drive of ¼ of the U.S. population. Nearly four million people visit the 762,000 acre, 1,200 square mile, WMNF each year to relax and enjoy the campgrounds, trout streams, ponds, and over 1,000 miles of hiking trails that are maintained here. Ranger stations are staffed to provide information about the area and other information is also available from the AMC and other facilities.

The WMNF has not always been here. Many environmental groups, and in particular the Society for the Protection of New Hampshire Forests, brought about the creation of the WMNF at the beginning of this century. It was recognized that the streams of New Hampshire were being polluted by the runoff from the forests resulting from the uncontrolled cutting.

It is ironic that the WMNF that we have today is the direct result of private enterprise wasting the land and the lack of any environmental concerns 90 and 100 years ago. If the private lumber companies had been practicing good forestry management this national resource might not exist today in its present form. Equally ironic is the fact that in order to create the WMNF the government had to purchase back lands that had been sold to the private lumber companies in the previous century. In 1867 the State of New Hampshire sold 172,000 acres for $25,000. Federal, state and private initiatives have been necessary to recover this land and return it to the public domain. The initiatives are on-going. In recent years the Forest Service and private groups have researched and prepared a variety of reports discussing the future use and preservation of what is now referred to as "The Northern Forest"—the vast forested areas of Maine, New Hampshire, Vermont, and the Adirondacks in New York.

The WMNF of today is a managed and multiple use forest.

Some areas are reserved strictly for hiking and human enjoyment. Other areas of the forest, a renewable resource, are harvested by the forest products industry. Today the lumber is cut in a managed way to insure proper attention to the environment and to the future high quality of the forest, to provide diverse wildlife habitat, and to utilize the trees in many different ways, from wooden products to pulp. All groups today agree that tomorrows healthy forest is dependent on the proper care that is given to it today.

## WILDCAT MOUNTAIN            Elevation 4,397

Professor Arnold Guyot of Princeton gave this mountain its present name most likely because either Guyot or a friend saw a wildcat while walking here. Prior to that, it had been known as East Mountain because of its location, east of Pinkham Notch.

There is a story that this mountain was once named Mt. Hight, a name that is now found on another mountain to the north. (See Mt. Hight.)

## WILLARD, MT.            Elevation 2,804

Mt. Willard is a spur of Mt. Field on the western side of Crawford Notch. The 19th century books provide different accounts for the naming of this mountain. Jonathan Willard was a hunter who spent most of his time in the Kilkenny wilderness and the Pilot Range. On one occasion, he reportedly named this mountain after himself. (In the Pilot Range, both Willard Notch and Willard Basin commemorate his presence in that still wild region.) A second source states that Mt. Willard was named by Thomas Crawford after Joseph Willard, a guest at the Crawford House. There was also another hotel guest, Professor Sidney Willard, after whom the mountain may have been named.

172

Mt. Willard is only 570 feet above the site of the Crawford House. At one time there was a bridle path up to this point so that hotel guests could get to it quickly and easily. In 1869 the Mt. Willard Turnpike Company was formed to build a road from the Crawford House to the summit of the mountain. However, a road already existed and the purpose of this company was only to improve the existing road. There is no evidence that the company ever did any work.

**WILLEY, MT.**                                   Elevation 4,302

The Willey House site is located at the base of Mt. Willey in Crawford Notch.

Mt. Willey is named for the Willey family who died here in 1826. Samuel Willey lived here with his wife, five children, and two hired men. In 1826 New Hampshire experienced a long drought. On August 26th, when torrential rains drenched the mountains, the parched soil was unable to absorb the downpours and the Saco River rapidly rose and flooded its banks. It is thought that because of the height of the water and the landslides on the surrounding mountains the family abandoned their house, leaving behind an open Bible on a table. When a traveler passed through the notch several days after the storm, he found nobody at the house. A search party found the bodies of Samuel Willey, his wife, two children, and the hired men. The bodies of the other three children were never found. Had the family remained in their home they would not have perished, for the house, protected by a large boulder, survived the storm.

---

*The Willey House.* W. H. Bartlett from Howard & Crocker, *A History of New England*. From the author's collection.

# WILLEY, MT.

The same storm that claimed the lives of the Willey family ruined the road through the notch for 21 miles, washed out 21 of 23 bridges, and buried many of the fields along the stream with gravel, mud, sand, and trees.

After the tragedy, the house was opened to the public to view for 12½¢ per person. The Eastman guide disapproved of this when it wrote: "There is, however, nothing within the ruinous edifice of sufficient interest to warrant even this trifling expenditure."

This tragedy had a profound impact on the residents and visitors in the White Mountains. Dr. T. W. Parsons of Boston wrote a lengthy ballad describing the storm, the family, and their tragic deaths. Several of the verses are as follows:

> You see that cottage in the glen,
>     Yon desolate forsaken shed—
> Whose mouldering threshold, now and then,
>     Only a few stray travellers tread.
>
> A happy home it was of yore:
>     at morn the flocks went nibbling by,
> And Farmer Willey, at his door,
>     Oft made their reckoning with his eye.
>
> One sultry August afternoon,
>     Old Willey, looking toward the West,
> Said—"We shall hear the thunder soon;
>     Oh! if it bring us rain, 'tis blest."
>
> For down the mountain's crumbling side
>     Full half the mountain from on high
> Came sinking, like the snows that slide
>     From the great Alps about July.
>
> Old Crawford and the Fabyan lad
>     Came down from Ammonoosuc then,
> And passed the Notch —ah! strange and sad
>     It was to see the ravaged glen.

But having toiled for miles, in doubt,
>With many a risk of limb and neck,
They saw and hailed with joyful shout,
>The Willey House amid the wreck.

And still upon the lawn before,
>The peaceful sheep were nibbling nigh;
But Farmer Willey at his door
>Stood not to count them with his eye.

## WONALANCET, MT.        Elevation 2,800

Located south of Mt. Passaconaway in the Sandwich Range is Mt. Wonalancet. Wonalancet was the Indian Chief who succeeded Chief Passaconaway. After being defeated by the white settlers, Wonalancet led his Indians to St. Francis on the St. Lawrence River in Canada.

## ZEALAND MT. and Zealand Notch      Elevation 4,301

Zealand Notch is located to the west of Crawford Notch and south of the Rosebrook Range. There are hiking trails and an AMC hut in this area.

The origin of the name is lost to history. It may be a reference to New Zealand. What is remarkable about this area is how it has recovered from the huge forest fires at the turn of the century that ravaged the forests and greatly damaged the soil. A fire in 1886 destroyed 12,000 acres in this area. Before the forest had recovered, a second fire in 1903 destroyed 10,000 acres. In 1915, after the passage of the Weeks Act, the entire Zealand River watershed was purchased by the White Mountain National Forest.

# Artists and Photographers

The scenery of the White Mountains has been recorded by artists since the first painter visited there and transferred what he saw in the hills to the canvas in front of him. After the American Civil War when photography replaced paintings as a means to remember a visit to these mountains, the photographer became artist. Below are brief sketches about some of the artists, painters and photographers, whose works are included in this book. As the painters preceded the photographers to these hills, so they shall be first here.

## Painters

### COLE, THOMAS

Thomas Cole was 18 years old when he came to America from England in 1819. As an accomplished artist, he spent the summers exploring New Hampshire's White Mountains, the Catskills and Adirondacks in New York, and Mount Desert Island in Maine. During the winters Cole would return to his studio in New York to complete the works that he had started during the summer months. During the winter of 1848 Cole died at his home in the Catskills. Cole's spectacular paintings of the White Mountains caused other painters to go there to paint the same scenes and tourists to go to see for themselves the mountain scenes that he had put on canvas.

Color insert: *The Notch of the White Mountains (Crawford Notch)*, 1839. Oil on canvas, 40x60.5 inches. Andrew W. Mellon Fund. Photograph © 1992 National Gallery of Art, Washington. All rights reserved.

### HILL, EDWARD

Edward Hill was born in England in 1843 and came to America the following year. In 1871 Hill moved to Littleton,

New Hampshire with his wife. For the next several years Hill traveled extensively in this country before more permanently settling in northern New Hampshire. Between 1877 and 1892 Hill was the artist in residence at the Profile House in Franconia Notch. After the death of his wife in 1891 Hill traveled again to Europe and the American West. He died in Hood River, Oregon in 1923.

Color insert: *Presidential Range from Jefferson Highlands*, 1886. Oil on canvas, 30x50 inches. Photograph © 1992 by the New Hampshire HIstorical Society. All rights reserved.

## HOMER, WINSLOW

Winslow Homer began his artistic career as an apprentice in a lithographic shop in Boston in 1855. Becoming bored with this, Homer moved to New York where he did illustrations for *Harper's Weekly* and other magazines. After a while, Homer turned his attention to oil painting. In 1868 and 1869 Homer visited the White Mountains. In later summers, he visited the Adirondacks and Gloucester, Massachusetts. Homer's work includes two paintings of the Bridle path on Mt. Washington. In one, now in the collection of the Art Institute of Chicago, it is said that Homer included a self-portrait of himself in the foreground. The same girl with blond hair appears in both Bridle Path paintings and also in an illustration of the same scene published in *Harper's Weekly* in 1869.

Color insert: *Mt. Washington*, 1869. Oil on canvas, 16¼ x 24⁵⁄₁₆ inches. Gift of Mrs. Richard E. Danielson and Mrs. Chauncey McCormick. Photograph © 1992, The Art Institute of Chicago. All rights reserved.

## KENSETT, JOHN FREDERICK

John Frederick Kensett was born in Connecticut in 1816. When he was 24, Kensett went to Europe for seven years where he traveled widely and painted. Kensett first traveled to the White Mountains in 1850. His painting *The White Mountains, Mount Washington* shows the Presidential Range from the intervale and the meandering Saco River north of North Conway.

This painting was completed in 1869 and is an exact replica of an engraving, the original now lost, that was done for the American Art-Union in 1851.

Color insert: *Mt. Washington from the Valley of Conway*, 1869. Oil on canvas, 41x63⅜ inches. Collection of The Wellesley College Museum. Gift of Mr. and Mrs. James B. Munn (Ruth C. Hanford, 1909) in the name of the class of 1909. Photograph © 1992 The Wellesley College Museum. All rights reserved.

# Photographers

## BIERSTADT BROTHERS

Albert Bierstadt and his brothers, Charles and Edward, first published a collection of 48 stereographs in 1862. That book included a built-in glass prism to view the stereographic pictures. A second and better made edition of the book was published in 1875 containing 24 pictures. The Bierstadt stereographs are possibly the first photographs that were taken of the White Mountains.

## JONES, EUGENE S.

Eugene S. Jones began his career with the Boston and Maine Railroad in 1877 as a clerk and then became the Chief Clerk in the Car Services Department. Jones pursued his photographic interests purely as a personal hobby until he was asked by a member of the company's Claims Department to take some pictures of a train that had been involved in an accident. The Claims Department recognized the value of the photographic work, and Jones was assigned the responsibility of taking pictures for that department on a regular basis. Jones was later appointed the first official photographer for the Boston and Maine Railroad and was provided with a darkroom at company expense. He traveled extensively throughout New England and the White Mountains taking pictures for the railroad. During one year he reportedly traveled 21,980 miles taking over 1,200 pictures, half of which were for the legal department.

## SHOREY, GUY L.

Born in Gorham in 1881, Guy Shorey began taking pictures of the White Mountains in 1898 and became a prominent photographer of these mountains. Shorey had both a photography studio and a pharmacy in the town of Gorham. He was a lifetime member of the AMC, knew all of the mountain trails, and took panoramic pictures of the mountains with his large camera that used a 7"x17" negative. Many of his pictures were printed as postcards and sold throughout the area.

## SWEETSER, MOSES

The large and spectacular heliotypes included in Sweetser's *Views in the White Mountains*, published in 1879, represented an effort to provide the White Mountain visitor with a collection of pictures so that "fading memories may be refreshed, and pleasant associations revived" of northern New Hampshire. As originally published, these pictures were 8½ inches by 10 inches. In showing pictures of the hotels with the logged hills behind them, the Sweetser book accidentally provides a historic look into the logging industry and the barren lands that were left behind by that work. Sweetser also published popular guidebooks to the White Mountains.

# Selected Bibliography

In researching this book, I used many books, maps, and magazine articles. This bibliography lists only what I believe are some of the more important works. I have noted with an asterisk (*) those books that have been "recently" published and may be available in bookstores. Many of the other books listed will only be available in libraries or rare book stores.

*A. M. C. White Mountain Guide. The Appalachian Mountain Club, Boston. Various editions.

*Appalachia. The Appalachian Mountain Club. Volume I, Number 1—Volume XLIX, Number 1.

Atkinson, Brooks and Olson, W. Kent. New England's White Mountains: At Home in the Wild. Stephen Lyons, Editor. The Appalachian Mountain Club & The New York Graphic Society, 1978.

Ayres, Philip. Commercial Importance of the White Mountain Forests. U. S. Department of Agriculture, Nov. 4, 1909.

Ball, Dr. B. L. Three Days on the White Mountains. Boston, 1877.

Barstow, George. The History of New Hampshire. Concord, NH, 1842.

*Belcher, C. Francis. Logging Railroads of the White Mountains. The Appalachian Mountain Club, Boston, 1980.

Belknap, Jeremy. Description of the White Mountains in New Hampshire. From the transactions of the American Philosophical Society.

Bierstadt & Harroun. Gems of American Scenery Consisting of Stereoscopic Views Among the White Mountains. New York, 1878.

Bliss, L. C. Alpine Zone of the Presidential Range. University of Illinois and University of Alberta, 1963.

Boardman, Harvey. A Complete and Accurate Guide To and

*Around the White Mountains*. Boston, 1859.

*Bolnick, Bruce & Doreen. *Waterfalls of the White Mountains*. Backcountry Publications, The Countryman Press Inc., Woodstock, VT, 1990.

*Bruns, Paul. *A New Hampshire Everlasting and Unfallen*. The Society for the Protection of N. H. Forests, Concord, NH, 1969.

Burt, F. Allen. *The Story of Mount Washington*. Dartmouth Publications, Hanover, NH, 1960.

Burt, Henry M. *Burt's Guide to the White Mountains and River Saguenay*. New England Publishing Co., Springfield, Mass., 1874.

Burton, Alma. *The Story of the Indians of New England*. New York, 1944.

Campbell, Catherine H., Keyes, Donald D., McGrath, Robert L & Wallace, R. Stuart. *The White Mountains: Place and Perceptions*. University Press of New England, Hanover, NH, 1980.

Chisholm, Hugh J. *Chisholm's White Mountain Guide*. Portland, Maine, 1880.

*Crawford, Lucy. *Lucy Crawford's History of the White Mountains*. Stearns Morse, Editor. The Appalachian Mountain Club, Boston, 1978.

Cross, George N. *Randolph Old and New*. The Town of Randolph, 1924

Cross, George N. *Dolly Copp and the Pioneers of the Glen*. George Cross, 1927.

Douglas, William O. "The Friendly Huts of the White Mountains." *The National Geographic*, August, 1961.

Downes, Anne Miller. *The Pilgrim Soul*. Lippincott, New York, 1952.

Drake, Samuel Adams. *The Heart of the White Mountains: Their Legend and Scenery*. Harper & Brothers, NY, 1882.

Eastman, Edson C. *The White Mountain Guide Book—Third Edition*. Boston, 1863.

Eastman, Edson C. *The White Mountain Guide Book—14th Edition*. Boston, 1878.

Evans, George C. *History of the Town of Jefferson, New*

*Hampshire 1773-1927.* Manchester, NH, 1927.

Farmer, John and Moore, Jacob B. *Gazetteer of the State of New Hampshire.* Concord, NH, 1823.

Fogg, Alonzo J. *The Statistics and Gazetteer of New Hampshire.* Concord, NH, 1874.

Goldthwait, Richard P. *Geology of the Presidential Range.* New Hampshire Academy of Science, Bulletin Number 1, 1940.

Hayward, John. *The New England Gazetteer.* Concord, NH, 1839.

*Hill, Evan. *A Greener Earth.* The Society for the Protection of New Hampshire Forests, Concord, NH, 1977.

Hixon, Robert & Hixon, Mary. *The Place Names of the White Mountains.* Down East Books, Camden, Maine, 1980.

Howard, Reverend R. H. and Crocker, Professor Henry E. *A History of New England.* Crocker & Co., Boston, 1880.

*King, Thomas Starr. *The White Hills: Their Legends, Landscape and Poetry.* Chuck & Andrews, Boston, 1871. Facsimile Reprint 1991 by Heritage Books, Bowie, Maryland.

Ludlum, Stuart D. *Exploring the White Mountains 100 Years Ago.* Brodock & Ludlum Publications, Utica, NY, 1972.

*McAvoy, George E. *And Then There Was One—A History of the Hotels of the Summit and the West Side of Mt. Washington.* The Crawford Press, Littleton, NH, 1988.

McGrath, Robert L. and MacAdam, Barbara J. *A Sweet Foretaste of Heaven: Artists in the White Mountains.* University Press of New England, Hanover, NH, 1988.

*McKenzie, Alexander A. *World Record Wind: Measuring Gusts of 231 Miles an Hour.* Eaton Center, NH, 1984.

Merrill, Eliphalet and Merrill, Phinehas. *Gazetteer of the State of New Hampshire.* Exeter, NH, 1817.

Milliken, Charles R. *The Glen House Book.* Cambridge, Mass., 1891.

Morrison, Steven. "Life on the Roof of New England." *Country Journal,* January, 1978.

Oakes, William. *Scenery of the White Mountains.* New Hampshire Publishing, Somersworth, NH, 1970.

Poole, Ernest. *The Great White Hills of New Hampshire.*

Doubleday & Co., Garden City, NY, 1946.

Powers, The Reverend Grant. *Historical Sketches of the Discovery, Settlement and Progress of Events in the Coos Country and Vicinity*. Haverhill, NH, 1841.

*Randall, Peter. *Mount Washington: A Guide and Short History*. Down East Books, Camden, Maine, 1983.

Roberts, Guy. *The Flume and All About It*. Littleton and Whitefield, NH, 1924.

*Robertson, Edwin B. and English, Benjamin W. Jr. *A Century of Railroading in Crawford Notch*. 1975.

Roth, Edward. *Christus Judex—A Travelers Tale*. Issac N. Andrews, North Conway & Boston, 1864.

Spaulding, John. *Historical Relics of the White Mountains*. Boston, 1855.

Stewart, Chris and Torrey, Mike. *A Century of Hospitality in High Places: The Appalachian Mountain Club Hut System 1888—1988*. The Appalachian Mountain Club, Boston, 1988.

Sweetser, M. F. *The White Mountains: A Handbook for Travelers*. Houghton Mifflin & Co., Boston & NY, 1891.

Sweetser, M. F. *Views of the White Mountains*. Chisholm Brothers, Portland, Maine, 1879.

Swett, William B. *Adventures of a Deaf Mute in the White Mountains*. Boston, 1874.

Torrey, Bradford. *Footing It in Franconia*. Houghton, Mifflin & Co., Boston & NY, 1901.

Town of Randolph Sesqui-Centennial Committee. *Randolph: 150 Years*. Randolph, NH, 1974.

Van Diver, Bradford B. *Roadside Geology of Vermont and New Hampshire*. Mountain Press Publishing, 1987.

*Vincent, Lee. *Ten Years on the Rockpile*. Concord, NH, 1973.

*Vincent, Lee. *Instant Legends from the Rock Pile*. Concord, NH, 1975.

Washburn, Charles G. *The Life of John W. Weeks*. Houghton Mifflin, 1928.

*Waterman, Laura and Guy. *Forest and Crag: A History of Hiking, Trail Blazing and Adventure in the Northeast Mountains*. The Appalachian Mountain Club, 1989.

Weygandt, Cornelius. *New Hampshire Neighbors.* Henry Holt & Co., NY, 1937.

Weygandt, Cornelius. *The White Hills.* Henry Holt & Co., NY, 1934.

Wight, D.B. *The Androscoggin River Valley.* Charles E. Tuttle Co., Rutland, VT, 1967.

Wignot, Richard Gordon. "I Remember Guy Shorey." *New Hampshire Profiles*, July, 1976.

Willey, Rev. Benjamin G. *Incidents in White Mountain History.* Boston, 1858.

# About the Author

John Mudge is a financial planner and small business consultant. A graduate of the Northfield-Mount Hermon School, Amherst College, and the Whittemore School of Business and Economics at the University of New Hampshire, he is a member of the Appalachian Mountain Club, the Randolph Mountain Club, and the Society for the Protection of New Hampshire Forests. He has visited the White Mountains regularly for the past 40 years and continues to visit and climb there as often as he can. Today he lives in Etna, New Hampshire.